Spirit Messages

Connect with Guardian Angels, Archangels, Spirit Guides, Animal Guides, Nature Spirits, Ancestors, Departed Loved Ones, and More

© Copyright 2025 - All rights reserved.

The contents of this book may not be reproduced, duplicated, or transmitted without direct written permission from the author.

Under no circumstances will any legal responsibility or blame be held against the publisher for any reparation, damages, or monetary loss due to the information herein, either directly or indirectly.

Legal Notice:

You cannot amend, distribute, sell, use, quote, or paraphrase any part or the content within this book without the author's consent.

Disclaimer Notice:

Please note the information contained within this document is for educational and entertainment purposes only. No warranties of any kind are expressed or implied. Readers acknowledge that the author is not engaging in the rendering of legal, financial, medical, or professional advice. Please consult a licensed professional before attempting any techniques outlined in this book.

By reading this document, the reader agrees that under no circumstances is the author responsible for any losses, direct or indirect, which are incurred as a result of the use of the information contained within this document, including, but not limited to, errors, omissions, or inaccuracies.

Your Free Gift
(only available for a limited time)

Thanks for getting this book! If you want to learn more about various spirituality topics, then join Mari Silva's community and get a free guided meditation MP3 for awakening your third eye. This guided meditation mp3 is designed to open and strengthen ones third eye so you can experience a higher state of consciousness. Simply visit the link below the image to get started.

https://spiritualityspot.com/meditation

Or, Scan the QR code!

Table of Contents

INTRODUCTION 1
CHAPTER 1: UNDERSTANDING GUIDES, ANGELS, AND BEYOND 3
CHAPTER 2: GETTING STARTED WITH SPIRITUAL AND PSYCHIC PRACTICES 15
CHAPTER 3: HOW TO CONNECT WITH YOUR SPIRIT GUIDES 30
CHAPTER 4: CONNECTING WITH YOUR ANIMAL GUIDES AND TOTEMS 41
CHAPTER 5: MESSAGES FROM NATURE SPIRITS 52
CHAPTER 6: ANGEL SIGNS AND COMMUNICATION 61
CHAPTER 7: RECONNECTING WITH DEPARTED LOVED ONES AND ANCESTORS 71
CHAPTER 8: COMMUNICATING WITH ASCENDED MASTERS 80
APPENDIX: SPIRIT MESSAGES – COMMON SIGNS AND SYMBOLS 87
CONCLUSION 94
HERE'S ANOTHER BOOK BY MARI SILVA THAT YOU MIGHT LIKE 97
YOUR FREE GIFT (ONLY AVAILABLE FOR A LIMITED TIME) 98
REFERENCES 99
IMAGE SOURCES 105

Introduction

Many people innately feel that certain realms contain an entire world hidden away just beyond the reach of the five senses. Snippets and blimps of that world will sometimes subtly come through, although they will rarely manifest in a physical, observable form. More often than not, the other side will communicate in ways that are noticeable on the inside by those who receive, usually via intuition. More overt messages and even visible symbols from that other realm do materialize, but it's only through higher understanding and practice that you'll be able to truly tune into such frequencies. At that higher level of understanding, you'll realize that messages from beyond aren't as rare as you once thought.

These spiritual messages can carry important insights that can provide guidance, reassurance, comfort, wisdom, or even communication from your departed loved ones. Such signs can be instrumental in helping you surmount life's hurdles, such as grief, uncertainty, and various other challenges. By understanding these signs, you'll be able to strengthen your bond with your ancestors and heritage while also harnessing strength from the elusive realm of spirits, universal energy, and all the unseen forces that keep life churning along.

This book will serve as your comprehensive yet detailed guide, empowering you to detect and interpret these subtle signs from beyond. It will provide you with theoretical knowledge about spiritual messages in all their forms, from the very basics to advanced spiritual and psychic communication. You will also be acquainted with an exhaustive list of signs, messages, and symbols, including their appearance, power, and meaning.

Beyond theory, this book will delve deeply into the practical side of spiritual communication, teaching you about various sources of these messages and techniques that'll help you read into them. You will find that spiritual messages occur in nature all the time and are waiting for you to unlock their meaning through techniques such as meditation, clairvoyance, mindfulness, and plain old intuition. By reading through the following chapters, you'll have become more grounded, spiritual, and reflective. The meditative practices and other techniques you'll become familiar with will also be valuable tools on your overall spiritual journey toward inner peace and balance, propelling you well beyond just the ability to receive spiritual communications.

Rituals, ancient symbols, guardian angels, psychic powers, and nature spirits are only some of the topics that will be covered. The practical exercises you'll learn about will be of interest and use to all spiritually curious individuals, whether they're complete beginners or have already dabbled in esoteric waters. Even though it exists mostly beyond the natural human senses, the hidden spiritual world that you'll dive into through this book harbors valuable lessons and benefits that will undoubtedly translate into your everyday life. Understanding what these messages have to teach can help you resolve emotional and spiritual problems. Still, it can be just as valuable in your other pursuits relating to work, relationships, health, and much more. As you'll soon learn, spirit messages are not entirely different from most kinds of regular, worldly information. *Yet, they require perceptive adjustments on your part if they are to be properly understood.*

Chapter 1: Understanding Guides, Angels, and Beyond

To develop the skills needed to identify and interpret spirit messages, you must first acquaint yourself with a few essential concepts in this area. These are spiritual connections that manifest in people's lives through various means, and they include a range of phenomena that sometimes most closely resemble spiritual entities that dwell in the world beyond. Such forces can be described as spiritual connections because they are the ones that usually come through and act as kinds of intermediaries between living people and other, unseen realms.

Spirits communicate through various forms.[1]

This chapter will provide you with a theoretical foundation to help you understand all the essentials of spiritual communication presented throughout the rest of the book. These include many different sources of spirit messages, including spirit guides, animal guides and totems, angels, and more. Across this book, you will find a mixture of concepts from different cultures, religious practices, and historical periods, all focused on communication with spiritual beings and the realms they inhabit. This opening chapter will also explore the basics of how communication with these forces functions before you can move on to practical steps in the following chapters.

Defining Spiritual Beings

There will be a number of different spiritual beings discussed in this book, which are the usual sources of spirit messages that come through from the other side. They all play different roles and can emit unique messages that carry meanings specific to these spirits and the way they relate to you personally. Needless to say, these spiritual beings aren't something that's readily visible to humans, but they represent interpretations of unseen sources of spirituality and wisdom, as described by various traditions across the world.

Understanding what these beings are and how their messages manifest in your life is essential to learning how to become more in touch with what they have to offer. These spiritual beings will be explored in more depth in their respective chapters later on, at which point you'll be learning about their nature and the practical ways of receiving their messages. The basic overview below will give you a definitive introduction to these concepts, which will also help you determine in advance the spiritual beings most likely to relate to you and your goals in spiritual communication.

Guardian Angels

Guardian angels are a type of spiritual guide that should be a fairly familiar concept in most cultures. Their defining characteristic is their personal relationship with the living person whom they protect and guide in life. According to most traditions, they are assigned, usually at birth, and while they might step back at times, they will be present at least in spirit throughout your life. Guardian angels are your benevolent allies who want you to be on the right path, and there can be more than one at work.

The protective dimension of their role is perhaps their most famous aspect, as guardian angels are believed to do their best to protect people from physical and other harm. Their spiritual messages are usually supportive and reassuring, as the feeling of their presence reinforces the idea that people have someone above who's looking after them. Their love and support are unconditional, even though they might sometimes take a backseat for reasons that are difficult for mortals to comprehend.

Guardian angels also transcend religion and, in various forms, they show up in almost all worldly traditions and orbit around you throughout your life regardless of where you were born. They are subtle spiritual beings that will hardly ever show themselves and will rarely communicate directly. Cryptic messages can come in through numbers or certain objects like feathers, but most of the time, a guardian angel's message will serve the simple purpose of reminding you of their presence. This alone can be a source of great reassurance and security.

Archangels

The main difference between guardian angels and archangels is that the latter are a more universal group of celestial beings. This means that they aren't assigned, and they will rarely have a personal relationship with a person. Instead, their protection and guidance are bestowed upon all human beings. Archangels also have identities that are clearly defined. Some of the most famous ones include Raphael, Michael, Gabriel, Uriel, Chamuel (Samuel), Azrail, and Jophiel. The level of reverence for these and other archangels varies across religions and Christian denominations, with Michael, Gabriel, and Raphael being the most commonly invoked in rituals.

These beings are the direct subordinates of God and, as such, they wield enormous power, with each of them having particular associations and skills, as you'll learn in detail later on. One of the most important strengths of the archangels is their omnipresence and apparent omnipotence, which means that they are able to communicate with many people across the world simultaneously. This accessibility is what makes archangel invocations very popular in all manner of spiritual practices, including communication. When you learn how to understand their signs and messages, archangels will become a source of strength, courage, inner peace, guidance, inspiration, and much more.

Spirit Guides

Serving as an umbrella term, the concept of spirit guides can be taken as referring to each or all of the spiritual beings discussed in this book. One of the later chapters will discuss what that means in more detail, but the main purpose of the term "spirit guide" is to separate those spiritual beings that guide and communicate with people from the many other entities out there. Angelic creatures, animal spirits, departed loved ones, and other beings discussed here are textbook definitions of spirit guides because people can understand them to a much greater extent than paranormal and other phenomena that defy human understanding.

One way to classify spirit guides would be to separate those that show themselves in the physical world and those that do not. Animal guides, for instance, exist in forms that humans can readily observe, unlike angels. There are many forms that spirit guides can assume, with this book focusing on the most well-known and important forms. Beyond classifications, spirit guides are a rather simple concept, as the term simply describes entities, energies, or spirits that exist to assist and provide guidance to living souls. Apart from guides, these spirits are also intermediaries that allow people to feel the touch of things beyond their physical realm. Some spirit guides are constantly present, while others show up at particularly decisive points in your life.

Animal Guides

Animals play at least some role in most religions, but certain traditions give these creatures immense spiritual importance. Concepts like "spirit animals" among numerous indigenous peoples in America or reincarnation in Eastern traditions are prominent examples of the importance of animals in spirituality. Abrahamic religions and their scriptures also abound in animal symbols and anecdotes. Still, the idea of animals being imbued with spiritual essence, at least in the West, can be tied mostly to Native American traditions. For many Native American tribes and nations, animals were given spiritual importance within the larger context of reverence for nature. This includes the firm belief that nature teaches and guides people.

Your spirit animal guide can be any animal that you're particularly attracted to.[2]

Animal guides can be as diverse as the animal kingdom itself, and, as a larger concept, animal spirit guides are universal in a similar way to archangels. However, different animal spirits carry unique symbolism and meaning, and one person's energy is usually strongly attracted to a specific animal guide. This attraction is felt in the distinct inclination you might feel toward a particular animal, such as an eagle, and how often this animal appears in your dreams. It can also be an animal that you frequently run into, seemingly by chance, while you can't help but feel that there is a reason or meaning behind these encounters. There are many ways to determine which animal is your guide, which will be covered later on in this book.

Nature Spirits

Similarly to animal guides, nature spirits or guides nurture the connection between humans and their natural surroundings. These guides are closely associated with things like healing, energetic purification, grounding, balance, and tranquility. They can also be referred to as elemental spirits. Nature spirits come in various forms, including beings that you can't see, such as fairies or inhabiting aspects of nature that exist in the physical world. The latter includes parts of the world other than animals, such as trees.

Nature spirits also relate to the four basic elements of water, fire, air, and earth. In all forms of spirituality that focus on connecting with nature, the elements are an absolutely essential component of countless rituals. The importance of the elements cannot be overstated because they make up the entirety of the universe that humans inhabit. The elemental spirit of Earth, for instance, will lend its power to plants while that of water will inhabit the rivers of the world.

Ancestors

Ancestors can be a source of strength even without direct spiritual communication because they often inspire while also eliciting a sense of belonging and continuity that transcends a single person's lifetime. For this and other reasons, ancestors and heritage, in a broader sense, have been the objects of spiritual exploration in virtually all cultures in history in some form or another. This sense of connection that stretches back in time provides meaning and an affirmative existential context for an individual, titillating the fundamental human desire to belong to something greater.

The role of ancestors in terms of spiritual communication can be to guide an individual or an entire community of people. The latter role is the reason why groups of people tend to gather around a shared heritage, acknowledging ancestors as a common thread that binds the community together. Strengthening and exploring your roots can be an immensely empowering pursuit, whether by reading, learning through oral tradition, or any other path. Spiritual communication will only intensify this process and allow you to harness the inspirational power of your ancestry on a much deeper level.

Departed Loved Ones

Departed loved ones are one of the most frequent points of interest for people diving into spiritual communication, especially beginners. The deeply personal bond people feel toward the departed loved ones they knew in life means that these spirits can provide a special kind of guidance and reassurance. Such connections can also be sought as a means of attaining closure and resolving residual emotional issues that you didn't get to address while your loved one was still alive.

Despite some negative connotations attributed to them by popular culture, the spirits of the departed aren't ghosts or malicious paranormal entities whose purpose is to torment the living. On the contrary, connecting with these spirits can provide comfort and important insights essential to improving your life. However, connecting with the departed should not interfere with the natural grieving process. It's about nurturing a spiritual and intuitive connection with someone you care about while processing the fact of their departure in an emotionally healthy manner. As counterintuitive as it might seem, establishing a connection with the departed can help you process grief. There are many other potential benefits to this form of spiritual communication, which only you can know based on your personal needs and your past relationship with the person in question.

What Is Spiritual Communication?

While spiritual communication is an expansive term, like many of the concepts that will be studied in this book, in essence, it's all about how the universe speaks to you. When you consider the universe as a system of different realms that are all intertwined by certain energies, you'll begin to realize that there is a particular language at play that you can learn and understand. It's about realizing that you, as a creature with a degree of your own spirituality and imbued with universal energy and life force, are constantly being guided and influenced by the invisible touch of other energies. In the context of this book, these energies take the form of spiritual beings or guides.

It might be a difficult concept to wrap your head around at first, but it's rather straightforward in essence. One way to look at it is through the concept of prana, which originates in the traditions of Hinduism and related religious practices on the Indian subcontinent. The idea of prana permeates yogic traditions, alternative medicine, martial arts, and some of the biggest religions in the world. You can consider prana to be an invisible energetic thread that intertwines all things in this universe, whether living or inanimate. It flows through you, other beings and objects, and all layers of reality. Because of its omnipresence and interconnectedness, prana is seen as a fundamental force of life that keeps the whole universe churning along.

As such, every person has one physical and one spiritual or energy body. According to Eastern teachings, the energy flowing through you vibrates at a certain frequency and converges at seven important centers in your body. These centers are known as the chakras, arranged vertically in a particular order and stretching from the base of your spine and up to your head. You will learn more about your energy body and chakras in the next chapter, but remember that the sixth chakra (Ajna or the "Third Eye") governs intuition. Located around your forehead, this chakra is all about perception beyond the five senses, especially through intuition, which is why it's such a popular concept among psychics. Because of this, you can consider your sixth chakra to be responsible for spiritual communication.

The vibrating frequency of your energy body is also noteworthy because these vibrations have a significant impact on the attraction or deflection of certain energies when they meet in the universe. Your frequency can affect how much you'll attract or project negativity and positivity, the kinds of people you'll find agreeable, and the kinds of spiritual beings that will be most likely to speak to you.

The Role of Psychic Abilities

In their broadest sense, psychic abilities include an expansive range of extrasensory powers that allow people to exercise some form of sensing beyond the usual range of the human limits of the five senses. These abilities aren't always related to spirituality. They can include supernatural methods of affecting the physical world through powers such as telekinesis or simply perceiving the physical world beyond visual range. There are countless other examples of psychic powers, but the one that relates most closely to spiritual communication is mediumship or any similar ability.

Everyone can try their hand at developing basic psychic abilities and, with enough practice, develop these skills to a certain level.[3]

A powerful medium or psychic is someone who possesses the skills necessary not just to receive and interpret messages from the realm of spirit but also to contact the other side. While psychic abilities are integral to advanced spiritual communication, not everyone will have such powers, and some people are naturally more predisposed to developing these skills than others. This is why a wide array of spiritual techniques, practices, and rituals are meant to enhance the ability of regular people to detect and understand spirit messages. With that being said, everyone can try their hand at developing basic psychic abilities and, with enough practice, develop these skills to a certain level. Psychic power is a mighty tool that will play a central role in all of your spiritual communication efforts if you choose to hone these abilities.

The "Four Clairs"

You'll learn more about the "four clairs" through the rest of this book, but the basic principle relates to the kinds of psychic abilities that are all about powerful intuition. All human beings possess at least a moderate level of intuition, and some are undoubtedly gifted in this regard. However, your intuition is a lot like the capabilities of your physical body, which means that it can be improved and strengthened through exercise. One way of doing this is to be mindful of and understand the four clairs. As per established practice, the four clairs include the following:

1. **Clairaudience,** usually described as hearing voices, refers to your ability to receive internally audible messages. Of course, clairaudience is vastly different from hearing voices as a consequence of mental health issues. These inner voices that transmit messages via clairaudience are characterized by calmness and familiarity, never causing discomfort.

2. **Clairvoyance** works similarly to clairaudience, except that it refers to visual messages instead of vocal ones, which usually come in the form of images. These messages can be specific images, scenes, or landscapes, and they are usually metaphorical in the sense that they serve as pointers toward a meaning that you will decipher.

3. **Clairsentience** is about recognizing feelings and what they mean. Feelings are an essential medium of spiritual communication, so there is always a lot to unpack in the things you feel. This is the most common of the clairs by far since virtually everyone is born

with some ability to feel emotions or internal sensations, even in their most basic form. Deciphering the messages that come in through feelings requires introspection, which is one of the pillars of strong intuition.

4. **Claircognizance** can be summarized as knowing. In a way, this clair refers to the information you can gather from your intuition, interpreting that information and drawing valuable, rational conclusions from it.

As you can see, the four clairs all feed into each other in some way and come together into one whole. That one whole is your intuition, and the four clairs are just one of the ways in which professional psychics and spiritualists categorize and systematize the practice of intuition. Each of the clairs can be improved and developed individually or along the other clairs, which you'll learn about in the next chapter.

Myths and Misconceptions

Across popular culture, urban legends, and media, there is an abundance of misconceptions and myths surrounding communication with spiritual realms. Due to various ghost stories and legends popularized through things like horror movies, spirit communication is often wrongly conflated with the paranormal, especially in a negative sense. The spiritual beings discussed in this book should not be seen as ghostly caricatures that haunt the realm of the living for nefarious purposes.

Communicating with spiritual beings is about tuning into an invisible realm that exists on its own plane of reality and learning to decipher the few signs and messages that come through. Intuition plays a major role in this communication, and your expectation should not be to conjure up ghosts or any other phenomenon traditionally considered paranormal. Instead of summoning entities for personal gain or any other reason, you'll learn to observe, listen, and understand. While these spiritual beings will hardly appear to you in a physical sense, your skills in spiritual messaging will allow you to intuitively feel their presence.

Spiritual communication is still an undertaking that should be taken seriously and never underestimated or conflated with simple entertainment. This isn't because spirit messages pose any kind of danger. The practices associated with it don't always have to be *too* serious, but spirit messages should be respected because they can carry tremendous meaning and value. The messages that you receive from the spiritual realm will seldom be frivolous or pointless as long as you learn how to fully comprehend them.

Another common misconception is that attempts to receive spiritual messages are dangerous and invite trouble. These fears stem largely from media and popular ghost stories, especially concerning spiritual communication, as approached in this book. Paranormal activity, whether sought or uninvited, has been known to cause discomfort and other problems for people from time to time, which is why it's important to distinguish the spiritual from the paranormal.

Other popular misconceptions state that spirit messages can only be received by using special tools such as Ouija boards. As you'll learn later on, communicating with particular spiritual beings can benefit immensely from things like altars and other props that can enhance your efforts, especially in rituals. However, the Ouija board is more associated with the paranormal and relates closely to communicating with the dead, which is just one aspect of spiritual communication. It also doesn't rely on intuition, meditation, or most spiritual rituals that will be covered in this book. Ouija boards started as a game and were marketed as such until popular culture and occult spiritualists in the United States gave them a whole new meaning. Intuition, meditation, and psychic abilities are much older and more established methods of contacting the spirit world, and Ouija boards are far from being a necessary part of the process.

Many people also equate spirit guides strictly with concepts like guardian angels, which needlessly narrows down the concept. It's the perception of each person having only a singular guide that watches over them and provides guidance. In reality, spirit messages come from many sources and can be found throughout the world, pointing to a much broader system of energies and unseen forces that work together or separately to provide a whole range of messages. While it would be a simplification of the concept, it would be fairly accurate to see spirit guides as a team of unseen forces, some of which might stick with you personally while others will come and go throughout your life.

Similarly, some people falsely see spiritual communication as a highly esoteric and exclusive practice that only a gifted few can unlock. In truth, you don't really need any special abilities to receive such messages, especially on a simpler level. More than special esoteric abilities, spirit messaging is primarily about knowledge and your ability to listen on a deeply intuitive level.

Being contacted by the other side also doesn't necessarily require you to enter some kind of special mental state, such as deep meditation. Spirit messages can and will come to you in your normal, wakeful state, even though meditation plays a major role in honing your ability to hear, see, and understand more of what you're receiving. The messages will also come in your dreams, or they can come in when you're out and about, running chores or working. There are very few rules on when, where, and how a spirit message might arrive. The only rule is that you must know what to look for and how to read it.

Furthermore, it's important to understand that being in contact with any kind of spiritual guide is not about relinquishing control of your life. These beings aren't there to overtly intervene in your life and make your decisions for you. Their messages and wisdom are subtle signs that can help you make the right call, choose your direction, or simply feel more peaceful and balanced. At most, spiritual messages will gently nudge you in the right direction, but you will always have to remain at the steering wheel.

Overall, it's important to manage your expectations and also put your mind at ease. Spiritual communication will not immediately solve your problems, but it also won't summon a frightening ghostly entity to terrorize you or anyone else. Like meditation or standard religious practice, communicating with spirits is primarily about finding peace within yourself, becoming more grounded, and firmly interlocking your own spirit with the greater cosmic interplay of energy and spirits. Whether you want a more personal spiritual connection with someone who passed away or the universe itself, there is nothing paranormal or dangerous about these practices. There is also no obstacle to any beginner who might want to use these teachings to live a more spiritual existence.

Chapter 2: Getting Started with Spiritual and Psychic Practices

Before you delve into the practical methods of reading spiritual messages, it's important to understand the value of laying down a strong spiritual foundation. The best way to do this is to learn about your energy and how you can develop your spirituality in a broader sense that relates to more than just spirit messages. This entails learning about basic spiritual practices like meditation, breathing exercises, and visualization. It also means strengthening your intuition by developing the four clairs.

You must be in tune with your own spirituality to be more versed in the spiritual realm.[4]

You don't have to be a spiritual guru to read spiritual signs and messages, especially if you use the techniques that will be discussed in subsequent chapters, but spiritual work can only enhance the process. The more harmonious your energy and the more spiritually balanced you are, the more the spiritual realm will be unlocked to you. This chapter will provide you with an introduction to general spiritual work, elaborate on the four clairs of intuition, and provide you with a few exercises that you can adopt into your daily routine. Spiritual work like meditation has a plethora of well-known benefits to mental, emotional, and physical health that will be a welcome addition to your life regardless of your efforts to communicate with the spirit world.

The Importance of Spiritual Foundations

For about as long as human beings have been able to think, they've been expressing interest in the spiritual side of their lives. Countless cultures and civilizations have all contributed their customs, interpretations, and traditions to the larger human effort to explore spirituality. As such, spiritual work is an incredibly broad term that can entail any number of practices that you find most agreeable. The native religion that's prevalent in your place of birth certainly offers many avenues toward the exploration of your spirituality, but in the age of information, you can learn about and incorporate many other traditions and teachings to enhance your spiritual life.

There are a few foundational spiritual skills that are worth mentioning, which you are encouraged to explore in much more depth. Apart from developing the four clairs, it's a good idea to explore various forms of meditation while also learning about the power and importance of visualization. Both of these concepts play prominent roles in some of the foreign practices that have recently gained a lot of traction in the West, such as yoga. Furthermore, spiritual protection and psychic defense are also worth studying to strengthen your spiritual foundations even further.

In terms of meditation, it's up to you to decide how deep you want to dive into its techniques. Meditation is a very broad term that includes anything from basic and beginner-friendly mindfulness exercises to advanced yogic practices that involve tremendous effort and knowledge. Fortunately, there are many ways to approach meditation, at least in its basic form, without being a yogic master or studying Eastern traditions in depth. A couple of simple exercises that will soon be discussed will help you in that regard. The main benefit of meditation, particularly with regard to spiritual communication, is that it will make you more present and aware. On top of that, it strengthens and cleanses your energy, reducing interference from unwanted sources and making spiritual messages clearer.

Similarly, visualization is another concept that's simple in principle yet instrumental in all manner of spiritual practice, especially when it comes to communication. Visualization is a powerful exercise in mental strength, usually incorporated into meditation and various rituals. One of the key goals of visualization is to create, shape, direct, and otherwise modify the energies that pass through you or originate within you. It has a lot to do with the power of intention and focus to manifest certain intentions from your mind into the real world.

Overall, there are many ways to purify yourself spiritually and strengthen your energy, and the best approach is to adopt a routine that best suits your goals and lifestyle. You can do this by strengthening and fortifying your energy or simply by achieving a higher degree of balance and inner peace. Regarding spiritual communication, your goal should be to reduce any factors of stress that negatively affect your energy to minimize interference. In the process, you'll sharpen your intuition, increase awareness, and establish a firm energy base for more sensitive work, such as spiritual communication.

The Energy Body

There are many ways in which spiritual practitioners have tried to explain concepts such as universal and personal energy over the centuries. One of these interpretations concerns something called the energy body, which is one of the foundational concepts in all sorts of esoteric, meditative, yogic, and other practices. Your personal energy can also be interpreted through the well-known concept known as the aura.

Being an expert on what your energy body is won't be a fundamental prerequisite for reading spiritual messages, but it will go a long way toward helping you lead a more spiritual life. The tips and exercises that will be discussed later in this chapter will be much easier to understand if you first get a basic idea of how your personal energy works, what it is, and what components it features.

If universal energy can be described through concepts such as prana, then the energy body represents you as a concentration of energy that exists and vibrates at a certain frequency. This vibration, susceptible to positive and negative changes, works as your personal energetic signature. It determines how you and your personal energy interact with the universe and many other forms of energy you'll come into contact with during your life. These include the energy of other people, objects, spaces, creatures, or pulses from other realms.

There are a few different interpretations as to how your energy body can be broken down and defined, although they all describe the same thing and usually involve some description of a system of various parts. For instance, you can see your energy body as having five layers, which are known as the "subtle bodies." The five subtle bodies of your energy each refer to a certain domain or aspect of your energy, including your physical and etheric bodies, emotions, mentality, and spirituality. One of the main goals of energy work and spiritual exercises is maintaining a fine balance among these layers and having them work as a harmonic whole. When in balance, the layers come together into a strong and healthy energy field around you, which can also be called your aura.

The chakra system is similar to the idea of the subtle bodies or layers in that it also places great emphasis on balance and harmony. Since the seven chakras are defined as energy nodes or points where your energy converges, they can also be seen as important channels of communication between your physical and energy bodies. As both prana and your own energy need to flow smoothly and continuously through the chakras, spiritual practices such as yoga and meditation attribute great importance to unblocking the chakras and keeping them clear.

The chakras.[5]

Keeping your sixth chakra (Ajna) clear is especially important for spiritual communication because of its strong association with intuition. This so-called Third Eye is what will allow you to see and intuitively derive meaning from spirit messages. For this reason, there will be a number of exercises throughout the remainder of this book that will focus on either strengthening your Ajna or using its power to enhance rituals and see the messages from spirit guides with more clarity.

Practical Spiritual Exercises

The following tips and exercises are all about strengthening your spiritual foundations and getting acquainted with basic spiritual skills. Developing these skills will help harmonize your energy and improve your overall well-being in your daily life, so they represent a broader set of skills that don't relate solely to spiritual communication. Some of these practices can also play direct roles in rituals and exercises that relate specifically to receiving and decoding certain kinds of spiritual messages.

Breath Awareness

Breath awareness or mindful breathing is a staple of meditation and yoga, especially pranayama yoga, which is built around "breathwork." This is because, in yogic tradition, the function of breathing is seen as the most basic way of channeling the energy of prana through one's body. This means that altering your breathing in certain ways or paying attention to it for the purposes of meditation can significantly affect your energy.

In practical terms, breath awareness works well as an overture to any spiritual exercise or ritual because it's a way for you to enter a state of relaxation. Basic breath awareness is as simple as it sounds since it just entails an intense focus on your breathing process. It's the simplest form of mindfulness, which aims to drown out background noise and distractions while making you completely present, attentive, and relaxed. This can work with any object under meditative focus, but breathing is the simplest method.

Simply find a peaceful and quiet place and make sure that you are as comfortable as possible by wearing loose, soft clothes and taking a simple meditative position. You can sit normally in a comfortable chair or on a soft cushion on the ground, where you can cross your legs, straighten your back, and let your hands rest on your thighs or knees. Begin by shifting your attention to your breathing without trying to breathe manually or automatically. How you breathe is not important. The goal is to become aware of your breathing without reading too much into it or trying to alter it in any way.

Make yourself the observer and focus on how air moves through your nostrils or how your lungs inhale and exhale. Stay focused until nothing except your breathing occupies your attention. You might find this to be more difficult than expected, but if you maintain such focus for long enough, you'll enter a state of basic mindfulness, and mental clutter will fade from your mind. With enough practice, you'll be able to practice mindful breathing without hiding away in a quiet place, allowing you to enter a state of relaxation when you're doing chores or running errands.

Grounding Meditation

Grounding is another simple form of beginner-friendly meditation, and it's focused on strengthening and nurturing your bond with nature and its energy. It's about figuratively rooting yourself via focused energy in the earth, which promotes feelings of harmony, stability, and mental clarity. You can ground yourself in various ways and places, but natural settings are clearly the best choice. Grounding is meditative, but it's not a specific exercise with rigid instructions. Although it's meditative in nature, it doesn't always have to entail an actual meditation ritual.

Meditating in a forest or by a lake naturally entails grounding, but grounding also occurs through a number of other outdoor activities. Taking a long, lonesome walk in the woods while engaging in some basic mindfulness can be a grounding ritual. Essentially, you can create whatever routine or exercise corresponds to your personal preferences, and it will constitute grounding as long as it makes you feel closer to nature and relaxes your mind and spirit. The goal is to be at peace and develop a clear awareness of belonging in the natural world. In that sense, you can ground yourself at the park or even at home and enhance this feeling through simple adjustments like walking barefoot.

Energy Alignment

Aligning your energy means attaining balance and harmony within yourself, which can be achieved by any number of means. The preferred method will depend on the kind of problem that's causing instability in your energy, such as blocked chakras, negative energy attachment, and many other issues. Affirmations, visualization exercises, gratitude rituals, regular yoga, and meditation are only some of the methods applicable to energy alignment.

Beyond spiritual exercises, it's important not to neglect your physical health. A healthy body is home to a healthy spirit, which means that the state of your energy has a lot to do with how you're doing physically. It's no accident that many traditions in Eastern alternative medicine treat physical and spiritual health as inseparable, such as by approaching health issues through the chakra system. The process works both ways, so if you're feeling spiritually unstable or energetically diminished, it could be a simple matter of introducing healthy routines and habits into your life. This means regular exercise, outdoor activities, and especially dietary adjustments.

Third Eye Meditation

Meditating with a focus on your Third Eye is simply about growing your awareness of the sixth chakra and focusing your energy on it. The goal is to clear and strengthen the Ajna so that it enjoys a free and uninterrupted flow of energy that will allow it to function at peak capacity. Such meditation is aimed at empowering your intuition via your Third Eye chakra, which can be done in a number of ways. Keep in mind that meditating on your sixth chakra doesn't necessarily mean "activating" the Third Eye.

A simple meditation to rejuvenate the Third Eye starts with a certain intention, such as cleansing the sixth chakra or infusing it with fresh energy to prepare it for the intuitive aspects of spiritual communication. After that, assume your most comfortable meditative position and make sure to keep your back straight. The meditation should begin with a yogic breathing exercise meant to alternate between relaxing and tensing your body.

Breathing exercises strengthen your third eye.[6]

Inhale a deep breath and hold it while tensing the muscles across your body and counting to six. At the six-second mark, exhale the air in two parts with a tiny pause in between, making sure that the first exhale is shorter than the second. As you carry out this double exhale, relax all the muscles in your body. This process should be repeated three times, and remember to keep your intention in mind. This breathing exercise is a meditation in itself, but it can also be just an introductory part of a more complex meditation.

You can complement this exercise with something called the "expanding the gaps exercise." As usual, take a comfortable meditative position and straighten your spine, once again focusing on your breathing. The exercise is similar to basic breathwork in that you'll just be observing your natural breathing pattern, with the addition of a simple mantra like Om. The key difference is that your focus will not rest on the breathing itself but on the short intervals right between exhaling and inhaling. Stay still and simply observe the gap as it naturally occurs without trying to create or extend the gaps.

After these stages, you can move on to basic visualization focused on your Third Eye. With your eyes closed, try to internally look upward toward your sixth chakra without too much tension in your eyeballs, focusing on the mental image of your Ajna as it pulsates above your eyebrows. You should stay focused on the Third Eye and visualize peaceful energy flowing through it, spending up to ten minutes in a state of meditative breathing and relaxation as you utilize your mantra.

White Light Visualization

This visualization or meditative exercise focuses on visualizing and using something called white light. A common visualization technique, white light is used for spiritual defense, cleansing rituals, fighting negative energies, and much more. It's a concept with a wide application that you can incorporate into many rituals because of its simplicity in principle, with the point of creating and directing energy toward a particular goal.

For example, white light can be visualized to create a protective energetic layer that will have cleansing and fortifying effects on your energy. While this exercise requires powerful visualization, the ritual itself can be quite simple. All you have to do is enter a meditative state and begin visualizing a powerful white light by using real-world examples as a reference. Conjure up a mental image of things like snowy landscapes on a sunny day or sunlight dancing on water. Make it your intention to absorb this light as a protective force whose power will be used to make your energy stronger.

Picture the enveloping glow of this white light descending upon you from above and concentrating all around you. While continuing your meditation, try to visualize the white light and the air around you morphing into one field of energy. Use your breathing to inhale this energy and focus on the sensation of the air entering your lungs and diffusing throughout your body, visualizing the energy of white light entering every fiber of your body and spirit. Visualize your energy body and how it feeds on the white light that you're absorbing, becoming more radiant and stable in the process.

Sacred Space Visualization

This is a visualization exercise because it's all about creating a figurative space within your mind. This mental place is where you can go when trying to communicate with your spirit guides or engage in any other spiritual practice, especially meditation. Even though you'll be creating a mental sanctuary, it's still necessary to find a calm physical retreat for such exercises, too, such as a tranquil garden or a particularly comfortable and quiet place in your home. It doesn't matter where the place is as long as it inspires feelings of safety and calm.

To create a sacred mental space, you only need to position yourself comfortably and eliminate all distractions, especially electronic devices. As always, focus on your breath as you close your eyes and begin visualizing the air you breathe as a torrent of rejuvenating energy that fills every fiber of your being, both spiritually and physically. As you exhale, visualize the breath carrying all tension and stress outward, removing it from your body. Banish everything but the present moment from your mind, and picture yourself occupying a place tucked away in the deep recesses of your mind where no outside interference can touch you.

Picture this as a place where nobody but you and your spirit guide can enter, seeing it as a retreat where you'll come back whenever you need to. It's an escape where you and your spirit guides can bond and where you come for their guidance. Assure yourself fully that the entire universe has guided you to this place and moment so that you can unveil the world that exists beyond your senses, all with the goal of meeting your spirit guide. It can take a lot of practice to develop your visualization skills to such a level, but after some persistent repetition, you'll start to feel detachment from worldly affairs and problems or even your physical surroundings. This is when you'll know it's working, and your withdrawal into this sacred mental space will become a powerful tool to guide yourself into meditation, as you'll soon learn.

Third Eye Activation

Imbuing your Third Eye with peaceful energy and cleansing its chakra, if practiced long enough, will put you in a position where you might be able to figuratively activate your Third Eye. This is best done via various visualization exercises, which can be incorporated into your other meditation exercises or practiced on their own. The purple lotus visualization, for instance, is a common exercise with the potential to greatly stimulate your Third Eye.

The purple lotus is a simple visualization that relies on powerful symbolism. All you have to do is close your eyes during meditation and place your focus on the Third Eye as you would in previously discussed exercises. Once you're aware of the chakra and its location in your head, gradually shift your focus toward visualizing the image of a purple lotus flower emerging right where your Ajna is. Picture it as an opening flower featuring eight petals, representing your Third Eye and the action of opening it. Focus intensely on this image for at least a few minutes until you can vividly observe the image in your mind.

You can also use colors to visualize the activation of your Third Eye by imagining a simple dot in the middle of your visual field. Visualize it as a purple dot to potentiate its energy by using the color related to the Ajna. Visualizing this dot with your eyes open represents a more advanced level of this exercise, so you could begin with your eyes closed and slowly work your way up to the level where you can visualize at all times. Once you master visualizing the purple dot, you can try conjuring up more complex shapes in your vision. This kind of visualization is all about practice, and the more you do it, the stronger your visualization and intuition skills will become.

Developing the Four Clairs

As briefly mentioned earlier, your intuition, along with the four clairs, is something that you can develop on your own. Approaching intuition development through the four clairs allows you to categorize the work required into four separate chunks because each clair is associated with one aspect of your intuition. This makes it easier to build your intuition from the ground up and ensure that each component is as strong as the rest, giving them equal effort and attention.

1. Clairvoyance – Clear Seeing

Since clairvoyance is all about "seeing" with your intuition, it's naturally associated with the Third Eye or Ajna. Any exercise or meditation that you engage in with the goal of strengthening or activating your Third Eye will strengthen your clairvoyant abilities. You should treat your intuition just as you would a muscle, which means that the more you exercise it, the stronger it will get.

It's important to understand that, among humans, the ability to visualize is a spectrum. Some people have a natural gift of powerful visualization while others struggle to form images in their minds, but everyone can try to practice their visualization for some improvement. Beyond meditation revolving around your Third Eye, any visualization will function as a workout routine for your clairvoyance. A simple way to determine the power of your visualization is to observe the things happening in your mind when someone speaks to you. The information you receive from someone else should form certain images in your mind, and if it doesn't, you should make a conscious effort to form them. In the absence of aphantasia, which is the inability to visualize, your visualization skills will get stronger the more you try and create mental images to portray outside information.

Clairvoyance is all about "seeing" with your intuition.[7]

You can also form an exercise routine at home to strengthen your visualization and enhance your clairvoyance in the process. Take an inanimate object of your choice and place it somewhere in front of you, placing it in a way that ensures it won't move. Face the object, sit down, relax yourself, and focus intently on that object. Breathe smoothly and intensify your focus on the object as you gradually become aware of your periphery as well, but remain focused on the object.

While still looking at the main object, shift only your thoughts to the objects in your peripheral vision and all around you. No matter what you think you're seeing in your periphery, keep your eyes on the central object and only let your thoughts wander. Remain in this state for up to five minutes, and then write down everything you saw and how it made you feel. On paper, this is a simple exercise, but it will promote a stronger bond between the visual and the mental. After a period of repetition, you might notice that, in general, the images in your mind are becoming more detailed. You can try doing the same exercise in a setting you're less familiar with since you're likely to know your home very well, leaving very little room for imagination.

2. Clairaudience – Clear Hearing

While clairaudience is about "hearing" information within your mind, it's still profoundly connected to your physical sense of hearing. Apart from deafness, there is no sound-related version of a disorder like aphantasia. A healthy mind can still operate even if its ability to visualize is impaired or non-existent, but there is no disorder where you'll be able to hear selectively. Hearing can be diminished for some people, but they'll still experience a range of sounds if it's loud enough. As such, the simplest way to strengthen your clairaudience is to train your ears to be more sensitive in general.

This is best accomplished in a relaxing outdoor setting with as much natural sound as possible. Close your eyes so it's easier to focus on sound, reduce cross-sensory interference, and begin with breathing relaxation. With the intention of sensitizing your ears and deepening your psychic ability to hear beyond the physical world, focus as strongly as you can on making your hearing the main channel of input. Focus on as much detail as you can in the sounds around you, paying special attention to those sounds that you'd otherwise ignore. Try to unpack the soundscape into different layers or components while figuring out where each bit of sound is coming from. This will lend itself to imagination, so your visualization will be put to use as well.

What you want is to hear as much as possible while also developing your ability to discern as many different sounds as possible. Looking for layers in the sounds around you will make it easier to detect minute differences, which, in turn, strengthens your ability to intuitively tell sounds apart. As a result, you'll become more sensitive to both external and internal auditory cues. After a while, you'll gradually start hearing more than the average person, and it's only a matter of time until this translates into at least basic psychic abilities. As always, writing your observations down will enhance the exercise.

3. Clairsentience – Clear Feeling

The ability to follow your proverbial gut is one of the pillars of clairsentience. One way to enhance this clair is through basic exercises in empathy, especially those that mix in basic psychic abilities. A common exercise revolves around photographs of people, where you'll take a picture of someone you don't know while talking to someone who knows the person in the picture. Better yet, your partner could be someone who knows the person and has also taken the photograph in question. Observe the photograph and try to deduce as much as you can about this unknown person via your gut feeling alone. Focus on what kind of energy they're projecting in the picture, how they might be feeling, what they're like in general, et cetera. After a couple of minutes of guesswork, ask your partner how many of your guesses were correct.

On the physical side of clear feeling, energy-related exercises can boost your intuition tremendously. Any exercise that revolves around increasing your sensitivity to energetic shifts will do, including yoga, meditation, rituals against negative energy, and more. You should also learn as much as you can about your energy body, incorporating rituals that revolve around it into your daily routine. Advanced visualization exercises that have to do with energy, such as energy sphere visualizations, energy scans on yourself or others, and exercises related to your aura.

4. Claircognizance – Clear Knowing

Clear knowing is related to clear feeling because they both concern drawing conclusions from your intuition. They're both about trusting your gut, although clairsentience has a bit more to do with sensitivity to energies and is often focused on specific tasks or decisions that are at hand. In a way, it could be said that claircognizance is more chaotic. This is because it relies on thoughts, hunches, and instincts that seem to kick in at random.

Sometimes, you just have a "feeling" that you should or shouldn't do something, and it seems like little more than a hunch. Learning to trust this sense is essentially how you'll enhance your claircognizance. You can build up this trust by putting your intuition to the test, such as through the aforementioned empathy experiment with photographs. There are many other opportunities to test your claircognizance, however, and the more times your gut is proven right, the stronger it will become because it relies on the confidence you have in it.

Chapter 3: How to Connect with Your Spirit Guides

Now that you have a grasp on some basic spiritual concepts and practices and an understanding of what spiritual entities or guides are in essence, the path is open toward learning more about spirit guides. While reading their messages is often an intuitive exercise with many possible interpretations, many of these messages come in specific forms that have long been understood and studied by spiritual practitioners worldwide.

Connect with your spirit guides.[8]

This chapter will provide you with a more thorough understanding of what spirit guides are in general and what exactly their messages look like. You will also learn about basic techniques that will help you grow your sensitivity to spiritual messages and increase your ability to interpret them correctly. Knowing more about the role of spirit guides entails learning ways of identifying their presence as well, which naturally precedes the skills needed to begin communication with them.

Understanding More About Spirit Guides

As briefly mentioned earlier, the concept of spirit guides is a very general one, usually serving as the umbrella term to include all the different entities described in this book. Each type of spirit guide has its own specific definition, as discussed in the first chapter, but defining the general concept is a somewhat different exercise. Because the idea of spiritual guardians and entities that communicate with the living has been so prevalent across different cultures, there are quite a few interpretations of this phenomenon.

In the interest of simplicity, you should view spirit guides as entities beyond the physical world who are there to help people in various ways, usually with subtlety. Spirit guides can also be classified into personal and ubiquitous guides, also known as working guides. In some practices, each person is believed to have one personal guide, while other traditions, particularly Eastern ones, stipulate that everyone has multiple entities watching over them throughout their lives. At the end of the day, the exact number of personal guides that you have won't matter once you master the art of reading their messages, as these skills will undoubtedly allow you to reach out to all of them.

Spirit guides are not there to solve all your problems for you, but they can help you fulfill your potential, make positive changes, overcome spiritual or emotional hardships, and much more. If chance permits, spirit guides can even help those who aren't necessarily listening to them or actively looking for their signs. While fortune can extend its hand with great results sometimes, putting in the effort to learn the language of spirit guides is guaranteed to yield rewards.

All of the spirit guides briefly covered earlier have unique characteristics and purposes. They each play their roles and excel at different forms of guidance. This is one of the reasons why some of these guides are more subtle than others and why contacting some of them might be more challenging than is the case with others. High-level guides like ascended masters will require more skill, psychic prowess, and ritualistic sophistication than your personal spirit guide or a departed loved one. This is because your relationship with the latter benefits from an intense personal bond, which opens up opportunities even for untrained, amateur mediums.

While spirit guides are entities in their own right, a lot of their spiritual messages come through you. In other words, the communication between you and a spirit guide doesn't necessarily occur outside of you. The guides themselves are external, but your intuitive realization and understanding of their messages occur within you. In a way, you are the window and portal through which spiritual messages come in from the other side, and they ultimately manifest inside your mind. This is why intuition and introspection play such important roles in spiritual communication.

Another thing that's essential to understand about spirit guides is that they respect free will and will rarely, if ever, directly intervene in worldly affairs. You shouldn't expect them to solve all your problems or take the reins of your life. Still, that doesn't mean they won't intervene at all. Rather, it means that they have their unique, often subtle ways of intervening, which you might initially misinterpret as underwhelming if your expectations are unrealistic. A spirit guide's intervention consists primarily of guidance, spiritual support, and important realizations in your life. They can and will show up in times of great need or even at your invitation, but you must never forget that you will always be the one who's firmly in charge of your life.

Channels of Spiritual Messaging

Spirit guides have many different avenues of communication, and their messages can come in some rather unexpected forms. While interpretation is an exercise in itself, understanding the ways in which spirit guides communicate is essential because you need to know what you're looking for. On top of that, not all types of spirit guides will communicate in the same way, even though there can be a fair amount of overlap. Some signs and symbols are mostly unique to respective entities, and differentiating between them plays a part in understanding the message. In general, identifying messages from spirit guides boils down to knowing where to look, noticing the signs, and knowing the kind of entity behind the message.

For many people, spirit messages come in when they're dreaming. As spirit messages, dreams can also be classified into the broader category of visions, although different kinds of visions exist. Visions can occur when you're awake, although this occurs with far less frequency, and most people will rarely have such experiences. The definition of what constitutes a vision is also somewhat loose, although they usually entail some kind of distinct realization that manifests visually.

Waking visions can happen at random, but those who get them will often be highly spiritual individuals engaged in meditation or a similar exercise. On the other hand, dreams are ubiquitous and provide a window into spiritual communications that virtually everyone can access. Some folks will dream more intensely than others and not everyone will recall their dreams with the same level of clarity, but remembering and recording your dreams is a skill that can be improved with practice.

On the more subtle side of things, spirit guides will communicate through things like thoughts, feelings, and sensations. This is where skills such as the four clairs truly come into their own because recognizing these subtle messages requires significant introspection, self-knowledge, and intuition. For instance, recognizing that one of your own conscious thoughts is a spirit message instead of just another thought can be incredibly difficult for the untrained mind. Only those with advanced intuition and sophisticated introspective skills will be able to pick apart their own thoughts and analyze the nuances. With feelings and spontaneous physical sensations, it's a bit easier to identify that they're coming from a spiritual source, but your four clairs still have to be sensitive.

Spirit guides will also sometimes communicate through something called intuitive nudges. An intuitive nudge occurs when you experience a seemingly inexplicable yet distinct urge to do something. It can come in the form of a mysterious attraction toward a certain course or a thought that seemingly crops up out of nowhere and pushes you toward a particular path. This nagging feeling that something should be done is something that a lot of people experience, yet many of them don't know that it could be a message from their spirit guide. These so-called nudges are highly intuitive, as is the decision process that helps you determine whether this nudge should be followed or suppressed.

There are also spirit messages that are much more overt and observable, even tangible at times, representing a distinct contrast to abstract signs such as those in dreams or intuition. Spirit guides might leave signs and symbols in the most unexpected places, which can include actual ancient symbols from various spiritual traditions, as you'll learn in subsequent chapters focusing on specific spirit guides. However, the symbols can also come in everyday items, including feathers, crystals, personal items, and much more. Animals can also be incredibly powerful symbols and carry all sorts of messages, which is why it's no accident that animal guides represent their own category.

Symbols can also come in the form of everyday items, which include feathers, crystals, personal items, and much more.⁹

While symbols like feathers are associated with entities like angels, their specific meaning and that of other objects will depend on the context in which you encounter them and your personal relationship with those objects. Lost items might show up at opportune times or in ways that convey a certain meaning, which you'll intuitively perceive as meaningful. The same holds true for other forms of spiritual messaging, such as sounds, smells, and tactile experiences. All of these messages exist in the physical world and are thus perceivable via your five senses, but just like feelings and thoughts, they can be interpreted only through intuition.

Last but not least, synchronicities are a major channel of communication with spirit guides. These are coincidental events where you notice a peculiar pattern, repetition, or coincidence that seems so meaningful that you are convinced it couldn't have been an accident.

Thinking of a person just before you randomly run into them, having a brief vision of an event just before it happens, or having synchronized thoughts with someone are only some examples. Other synchronicities can include things like repetitive numbers, codes, colors, or anything else that seems to show up whenever you do or think a certain thing.

The ways in which these synchronicities appear are endlessly variable and can include anything that seems meaningful to you personally. Songs, phrases, sounds, smells, and many other occurrences can all be synchronous with other things in a way that gives you insight into what course you should take or reveal important truths. This is a textbook example of how a spiritual guide might be trying to get through to you.

Spiritual Communications and Connections 101

The exercises and tips discussed below will be foundational in allowing you to begin the process of spiritual connection. Think of them as entry-level skills and good practices that will be applicable to the more specific rituals that will be covered in the rest of the book with respect to specific kinds of spirit guides. These revolve around mental preparation, spiritual fortitude, meditation, and various routines that will enhance your receptivity to the spirit realm.

Setting Intentions

Your intentions will play a central role in all sorts of spiritual exercises. Whether in meditation, yoga, plain old prayer, or a complex esoteric ritual, setting a clear and powerful intention will be the driving force behind the effort. Remember that spiritual rituals are almost always about directing certain energies toward a goal, whether these energies are your own or external ones that you are trying to invoke and use. The intention behind the ritual is what you meditate on or use to visualize a desired result, which is why every ritual begins with an intention.

In spiritual communication, the basic intention is to establish contact with a spirit guide, receive a message, and have the clarity of mind and spirit needed to understand that message. Your intention should be firm, clear, articulate, and loving - or otherwise positive. The more positivity you project in your rituals, the more likely you are to attract a positive response from your spirit guides. The essence of the intention in the rituals you'll soon learn is to invite a spirit guide into your awareness.

Furthermore, intentions can be greatly enhanced in your rituals if you use things like affirmations, prayers, or mantras to articulate your intent. This is a way of verbalizing your goal to solidify its meaning and make it clearer both for yourself and the spirit guide you're trying to contact. Your affirmation can be anything you might think of, as long as it relates to the exercise at hand. For instance, if you're conducting a ritual aimed at receiving messages from a departed loved one, you can create your own special prayer or affirmation that resonates on a personal level.

Affirmations can also be conventional prayers or even excerpts from a poem, as long as they are relatable. One example of an affirmation directed at a spirit guide could be, "I invite my spirit guide to communicate with me for my highest good. I am open to your presence and guidance." This kind of verbal statement externalizes and clearly defines your intention, imbuing a ritual with powerful energy. Affirmations are used at the beginning of rituals or at various other points in the process, as you'll learn later when you go through some specific exercises.

Psychic Defense

To further solidify your spiritual foundation before communicating with guides, you could also look into techniques for psychic defense. Psychic defense and, similarly, spiritual protection are broad terms that describe an entire set of techniques and practices aimed at fortifying your spirit, energy, and mind against all sorts of negative influences. While spiritual communication isn't inherently dangerous, it doesn't hurt to build basic psychic defenses to make your mind and energy invulnerable to any potential interference. These can include false, unwanted entities like pseudo-guides or negative energy attached to you by other people, whether unwittingly or through deliberate psychic attacks.

It's about more than just protection because psychic defenses will inevitably accentuate your psychic abilities as well, helping you see spirit messages more clearly and understand them more easily. Basic psychic defense is very straightforward and can consist of simple exercises like meditation, daily affirmations, prayer, energy-cleansing rituals, and more. Aura shielding can be especially effective, allowing you to build a protective energetic layer around your aura to make your energy impervious to unwanted external effects. You can shield your aura by using shielding crystals that project a protective field, shielding visualizations, positive affirmations, and numerous other methods.

Physical changes in your lifestyle, such as healthy diets and regular exercise, can also strengthen your aura and will always have positive effects on your spirituality.

Meditation to Meet Your Spirit Guide

Trying to get in touch with your spirit guide through meditation is a common approach, and it'll depend on the power of your intention and your ability to visualize and focus. Refer to what you learned about sacred mental spaces in the previous chapter before you begin this process. Meditation to meet your spirit guide can be as simple or as complex as you wish it to be. It always revolves around visualization and mental effort, but the amount of time and effort you put into it will determine if it's a quick evening routine or a full-blown shamanic journey. The latter can also be conducted under the guidance of a professional psychic.

After you enter a state of relaxation and return to that special sacred place in your mind, you will have to engage in sophisticated visualization to get to your goal. Once you're in your sacred space, start by visualizing it, taking on a different, more complex form. Imagine a natural environment that inspires calm, connectedness, and beauty. Try to get as immersed as your mind is capable of, imagining the physical sensation of being there. Focus on specific details of this imagined space to make it feel more realistic, such as its colors, sounds, and smells. Imagine smelling the scents as you breathe in and out.

You can meet your spirit guides through visualization and focus during meditation.[10]

Next, imagine a path or stairway that leads upward to the sky, once again focusing on as many details as possible. These details can include visible things like divine light but also realizations and feelings, such as those telling you that this path leads toward discovery and enlightenment. Start a mental journey on this path and picture each step as bringing you closer to the realm of spirits and guidance, all while feeling a change in the surrounding energies.

Focus on the energy of this place as hard as you can and gradually visualize it turning into a feeling of some kind of presence beside you. Intensify this feeling and imagine yourself turning to your side, beholding a figure of pure blissful light and benevolent radiance. Imagine this as your spirit guide, and let each breath reveal a sensation of absorbing this loving energy. Try to attribute characteristics and traits to this figure, including wisdom, benevolence, compassion, and understanding. Focus on feeling a powerful personal bond to this being, making yourself feel as if you're greeting a lifelong friend or companion.

The only thing that then remains is to have a mental conversation and a spiritual exchange with this powerful entity. Ask the questions that trouble you and use your intuition to understand the answers. It's important to show gratitude as well, which you can do by visualizing yourself presenting a gift to your spirit guide or using a physical object as a ritualistic offering. The final stage of the meditation boils down to visualizing your way back home by following the same pathway you came through. Visualize your spirit guide following you as you leave and bidding you farewell until your next meeting.

As you can see, this is a complex meditative exercise that will require tremendous mental work and focus. The more steps you take to make your meditation more comforting and ritualistic, the easier it will be to rid your mind of distractions. Every time you finish such rituals, you should take time to reflect on the things you realized, felt, and thought, writing them down and analyzing the results. Allow yourself some time to let the impressions settle and become integrated.

Journaling

Identifying and understanding spirit messages often has a lot to do with recognizing patterns and referring to previous experiences when facing new information. Keeping a journal is one of the best tools available for these purposes. As briefly mentioned earlier, writing things down solidifies your thoughts, strengthens visualization, and makes it much easier for you to identify patterns.

Half the effort consists of writing in your journal, while the other half is about regularly studying your writings and referencing them as you try to identify new signs from your spirit guides. Your journal should focus on signs, symbols, synchronicities, feelings, random thoughts, or anything else you believe might be connected with a spirit guide. Since spirit message interpretation tends to be personal, only you will know, through your intuition, which signs are worth recording. Consider the following prompts as a general idea of the kinds of observations you should be making, in addition to writing down the details of your experiences in actual rituals:

Have I experienced any feelings today that seemed to come out at random, without a clearly identifiable source, and unrelated to any specific event?

Which of today's events felt peculiar in the sense that they seemed inexplicably connected to something else through sheer coincidence?

Did I encounter any objects that appeared in places where they didn't belong or somehow provoked an emotional response that felt meaningful for reasons that are difficult to explain?

Was my attention grabbed by any specific symbols I've seen, and how did they make me feel? What is the meaning of these symbols?

Automatic Writing

Automatic writing is a technique that can enhance a number of specific spiritual communication rituals while also having some more general benefits in your daily life. It's a simple exercise that revolves around unfiltered, non-stop expression through pen and paper for a certain interval. The nature of the exercise is such that it can provide a whole lot of text, so it's a good idea to designate a specific part of your journal or have an entire notebook dedicated to automatic writing.

After you prepare a pen and notebook, all you have to do is pick a theme that works best in the form of a question. The question should ideally be one that a spiritual guide might help you with, referring to the kind of guidance you need or the solution for a particular problem. Once you set the question firmly in your mind, you'll attempt to answer it yourself. Take a timer and set it to an interval of your choosing, perhaps no more than twenty minutes.

The moment you let the timer loose, start writing continuously, letting everything that comes to your mind onto the paper. Let your pen function as a free-flowing conduit to every thought, impulse, idea, or feeling that your mind might conjure up, and try to let your brain wander as much as possible while keeping your question in focus. Try not to think about what you're writing, and don't try to keep the grammar or punctuation clean. You want to produce a torrent of spontaneous thoughts that are externalized on paper in as raw of a state as possible. Once you're done, you should take some time to analyze your writing.

Try to understand how some of the thoughts formed and where they came from. The exercise aims to let your intuition run wild and learn how to trust it. Automatic writing can also do wonders for your claircognizance by strengthening your so-called gut feeling. You should also try to identify which of the thoughts in your notebook were conscious and which weren't. Among the latter is where you're most likely to find a message from a spiritual source. As a result, automatic writing will also improve your ability to differentiate between your thoughts and those incepted by your spirit guides.

Strengthening the Connection

As with any other spiritual practice, communicating with your spirit guide will benefit greatly from the regular effort that's incorporated into some sort of routine. This includes rituals aimed specifically at spiritual communication as well as general exercises to keep your energy in balance. Morning routines can be especially important because they can set the right mindset that will positively affect the rest of your day. As you learn about more rituals throughout the rest of the chapters, you'll be able to decide which rituals concerning your spirit guides are the simplest or most applicable to your usual routine, allowing you to create a tailored approach that best suits your needs.

In general, it's good practice to begin your day with at least some basic meditation involving breath awareness and brief check-ins with your spirit guide. Grounding meditation is also an excellent way to start your day if your living conditions and location allow it. You should also remember to practice gratitude throughout your day in whatever way you see fit, particularly toward your spirit guides. Small symbolic offerings or meditative reflections at a basic altar dedicated to your spirit guides will deepen your bond and facilitate a healthy and positive mindset.

Whenever you can, take a moment to reflect on the guidance you have already received from the spirits, expressing gratitude for it and a hope for their continued assistance in the future.

Chapter 4: Connecting with Your Animal Guides and Totems

Now that you've got a solid grasp on basic spiritual work and the essential concepts behind spirit guides, it's time to delve deeper into the various forms that spirit guides take. This chapter will focus on animal spirit guides and the adjacent topic of animal totems, which feature various similarities but also a number of key differences. Both of these separate concepts include powerful symbolism and revolve around the inherent human connection to facets of the natural world, in this case, animals.

Spirit guides can come in an animal form.[11]

Across this and the following chapter, you will find that nature abounds in spirits, messages, and guidance, waiting to be unlocked by a spiritually curious mind. You will soon learn more about what animal guides and totems are, what messages they might have for you, and how to read them. These mighty spiritual allies that assume the form of animals are diverse and are always at work to help people, but you have to know how to listen to their guidance.

Animal Guides and Totems

One of the key differences that set animal guides apart from other spirit guides is that they can take a form that's clearly observable in the physical world. Even if they are encountered indirectly, such as in a dream or vision, animal guides still assume a form that's familiar to the human mind. Animals are an essential part of the natural world and, as such, have played many crucial roles in the human experience since the very beginning.

This deeply rooted familiarity is what has facilitated a certain level of understanding that humans have for animals despite the many ways in which they differ from each other. It has also imbued animals with great importance in the lives of people, which has translated into spirituality time and time again. Animals act as powerful symbols, and how they look, behave, and interact with humans has always been given a lot of meaning across different cultures.

The first step toward harnessing the power of animal guides and totems is to understand what makes them different. As briefly mentioned, a spiritual animal guide can be seen as an entity that takes the shape of an animal to convey certain meanings to people. As an entity that resides in the spiritual realm, an animal guide might come into your life in specific situations or when you're facing a particular challenge. Animal guides can communicate warnings, lessons, and all manner of wisdom, often related to the natural traits and instincts of the animal in question.

On the other hand, an animal totem, sometimes also referred to as your power animal, should be seen as a lifelong companion and protector, meaningful to you on a deeply personal level. The concept of animal totems is usually associated with Native American culture and is steeped in thousands of years of tradition that's intensely focused on the human spiritual relationship with nature and the animal kingdom. Your animal totem or power animal is your personal natural protector and companion that serves as a conduit between you and nature, symbolizing some of your essential characteristics. It can be a symbol of your essential identity and spiritual power and is tied to your deepest values and the path you walk in life.

As a symbolic representation of your essence in animal form, your animal totem can be interpreted as your spirit and essential self. As per some Native American traditions, an individual can have as many as nine animal totems. Discovering your personal animal totems is a deeply introspective exercise in which you must be sensitive to how you feel and think about certain animals. Experiences with those animals can also be meaningful and indicative of a special relationship. If a certain kind of animal seems to follow you everywhere you go, whether in dreams or in your waking hours, it might be your power animal. Being spontaneously approached by such an animal and being shown trust by them is also a powerful confirmation of a bond.

As your highly personal symbol or emblem, your animal totem's meaning can be quite flexible. Across cultures, different animals have their unique, innate symbolisms, but an animal totem's essential power is still in the way it relates to you personally. For instance, dragonflies are generally seen as signs of good luck, while butterflies often represent transformation and change, but that doesn't mean they'll necessarily represent the same things for everyone. The main importance of your animal totem will be in the traits, strengths, weaknesses, and inclinations that you and that animal share.

How Animal Guides Communicate

In regard to animal spirit guides and how they might communicate with you, there will be some signs that they share with other spirit guides. Other signs will be specific to the animal kingdom as a whole or to individual animal species. As mentioned earlier, recurrence is an essential sign. The more often you see an animal, whether in person or in a vision or dream, the more likely it is that an animal guide is trying to communicate with you.

These animal spirits might appear in their full form, but they can also communicate through traces hinting at their presence. The animal guide's choice between the former and the latter can also hold a meaningful message in itself. For example, repeatedly seeing a hawk or just finding its feathers without seeing the actual bird can be an important distinction. An animal spirit guide might have its reasons for being intentionally elusive toward you while deliberately leaving a trail of small hints to let you know that they are present. Bits of fur, horns, or tracks are also common signals with which animal spirit guides can communicate, indicating that you are following their trail in the wild or that they routinely visit places where you often find yourself in life.

To identify animal guides and understand their messages, it's also crucial to understand the behavior, habitat, and other natural characteristics of individual animals. Knowing these things will make it easier to discern whether an animal's presence in a given location is a mere coincidence or something more. The same goes for the symbolism of different animals across spiritual traditions, which you should extensively study once you identify which animals tend to make a recurring entrance in your life.

For example, consider how an owl lives and what it represents. An owl is a nighttime hunter who tends to dwell in forests or near them, symbolizing things like wisdom, powerful vision, and intuition in many cultures. If you find yourself taking an evening walk on a forest trail and you hear or see an owl, this may or may not be a meaningful encounter. On the other hand, if an owl visits your suburban home at noon or – *stranger yet* – shows up in an urban environment, the likelihood that this is just chance will be much smaller.

Because of its strong association with wisdom and insight, a spirit guide in the form of an owl might emerge at a time when you need guidance and wise reflection regarding an important decision. Taking into account the place and time of this encounter, as well as the thoughts and feelings that it sparks within you, such a meeting could produce an intuitive nudge or overtly reveal to you the path that you should take. The combinations of circumstances and subtle signs that might accompany an animal encounter offer a virtually limitless array of ways for spirit guides to communicate via animals. At the end of the day, the true meaning behind these encounters will only be unlocked through your own intuition and deep reflection.

Connecting with Animal Guides

To understand the messages you might be getting through animal guides, you'll generally analyze physical encounters with certain animals or read into synchronicities associated with those animals. Animals might appear repeatedly not just as a physical presence but also as images, visions, dreams, or thoughts. Apart from passively observing and analyzing such clues, you can also take a more proactive approach through some of the exercises described below.

Connecting via Meditation

As is often the case, meditation is a powerful venue for wandering into the spirit realm, and it's no different with animal spirits. However, connecting with an animal guide via meditation can be particularly tricky and requires a fair amount of practice. This is because the skittish nature of animals can often carry over into their spirits as well, so they aren't always rushing to talk to people.

As always, the meditation starts with an intention; in this case, the idea of having an animal guide reveals itself. This can be the spirit of an animal that fascinates or frequently visits you, or it can be the spirit of a departed pet. After setting your intention, you will move on to your usual meditative position and begin a process of visualization. Don't set high expectations or overthink the process, and don't try to analyze what you see. The goal is to simply conjure up the animal in the eye of your mind.

Connect to your animal guides by meditating.[12]

Visualize a walk along a path in the forest or somewhere else that's comfortable and serene. Without analyzing anything, let the sights, sounds, and smells of this place conjure up in your mind, and just observe. As you walk down this path, imagine that you are coming upon a place of transition into the realm of spirits. This can be a doorway, bridge, or anything else that symbolizes crossing over to another side. Before crossing over, reinforce your intention to meet an animal spirit guide and formulate it as a humble request. Assure yourself that a guide wants to meet you and will be waiting on the other side, and then gradually cross.

Visualize yourself coming across a figure in the distance, fitting seamlessly into a natural landscape before you. Imagine this figure as small and distant at first – but gradually getting closer. This will be your animal guide.

As the meeting draws nearer, visualize more and more details of this ethereal animal and allow it to dictate the tempo of the encounter. Depending on the kind of animal guide you're meeting and your goals, you will, at this point, ask the questions that you want to ask, all while maintaining an intense meditative state.

Animal Guide Journaling

Like most other forms of spiritual communication, keeping a journal can greatly help. It will help you keep a record of all suspected spirit messages, whether real or not, and allow you to reference them in retrospect. This is essential if you are to notice the patterns and synchronicities that so often accompany these messages. It's all about collecting as much data as possible and then processing it gradually. The more things that you write down, the more nuanced and perceptive your efforts at identifying animal guide messages will become.

A journal or a part of a journal dedicated to animal guides would be rather simple. Your main focus would be on recurring symbols, signs, and encounters associated with animals. The animals that hold a higher degree of meaning for you should get the most attention, of course, but any recurring instances can be important even if they don't feature the animals that you're most interested in.

You can start by making a journal note of every time you see a symbol or sign connected to an animal or any physical encounter, for about a month. When you start writing everything down, you'll find that many instances in daily life are brushed off or simply forgotten, making it more difficult to identify patterns and recurrences. Writing down every instance and reviewing your journal every day is the quickest way to figure out which animals are repeatedly showing up in your life.

As always, make sure that you also record the things you felt or thought during particular encounters. When you review your journal thoroughly at the end of the month, you might find that certain animals show up quite frequently and are accompanied by sensations, feelings, thoughts, intuitive nudges, and much more. If you notice repetitions both in the encounters and the accompanying features, you can be fairly certain that an animal guide is at work.

Using Animal Oracle Cards

Animal oracle cards can be of great use as a means of drawing hints and inspiration from the animal world, but they can also help you identify which guides you are most inclined toward. These cards, which can be bought or even made if you're feeling creative, mostly revolve around animal symbolism and are meant to explore your connections with certain animals. All you need is a deck of oracle cards, a quiet space, and a journal where you can document your discoveries and messages. The main benefits of using animal oracle cards include strengthened intuition, emotional processing, and life insights.

The simplest way to use a deck of oracle cards is to sit down in your meditative space and set an intention, usually a question or an issue where you need guidance. Focus your energy on your objective and shuffle the deck while continuously reflecting on your intention.

Once you've thoroughly mixed up the cards, you can draw a card and see what it tells you. You can draw this card at random or try to intuitively feel which card you're most drawn to, and you can repeat this process with multiple cards for a more detailed reading. To use your card deck to identify which animal's spirit resonates with you the most, it's a good idea to indulge in some repetition to see which animal card seems to show up more than others.

You can try different spreads and layouts for a more complex reading, such as a basic three-card spread. This spread is frequently used to gain insights into your past, present, and future, which the three cards will represent. The idea is to interpret how the past connects to the present and influences your current circumstances and the events yet to come.

Getting in Touch with Your Animal Totem

Connecting with your animal totem is all about identifying it and strengthening your bond with that particular animal symbol. It's an exercise in reflection, introspection, meditation, prayer, and much more, with the ultimate goal of drawing inspiration and spiritual strength from your power animal. As such, it's a spiritual endeavor that's considerably different from receiving animal guide messages because it boils down to finding a bond that already exists and then exploring it for your spiritual benefit.

The main benefit of intensifying the bond with your animal totem is that it'll help you align with your spiritual path and, hopefully, unlock hidden strengths and qualities within you that you didn't know existed. It's all about honoring your animal protector and getting in touch with the traits and strengths that this animal symbolizes through its nature and characteristics. Below, you'll find a few examples of how you can deepen this connection with an animal totem and, by extension, nature as a whole.

Animal Totem Quest

An animal totem quest, in this case, a shamanic journey through the spirit world, is a fairly complex meditative exercise meant to help you meet your animal totem and strengthen the bond between you. It's about journeying through the three main spirit worlds of shamanic cosmology, which include the lower, middle, and upper worlds.

These three worlds are usually interpreted as making up the proverbial tree of life and representing the tree's roots, trunk, and branches, respectively. The lower world is the residence of animals and other nature spirits, in humans associated with the unconscious mind and psychology.

Animal totems.[13]

The middle world is the realm of human beings, both those who are alive and those whose spirits refuse to move on to the spirit realm. It's associated with basic survival instincts but also the human desire to transcend and find meaning in the universe. Lastly, the upper world is the world of higher spiritual entities, especially guides like angels, the ascended masters, and other high beings.

To take this shamanic journey, you should try and induce a trance-like state, which is the basis of many shamanic rituals. This is usually done with a set of drums because rhythmic drumming, particularly at a rate of three to four beats per second, facilitates a state of trance. The same holds true for a variety of repetitive sounds, but drums are the traditional tool of choice for shamans. Doing the drumming yourself will be more immersive, but recordings of shamanic drumming found on the Internet can do the trick as well. Inducing a shamanic trance is no easy task for beginners, of course, so it will require a lot of practice and intense concentration.

The journey is best done by lying down comfortably for up to 30 minutes immersed in shamanic drumming. You can conduct this ritual in darkness or cover your eyes to minimize distractions.

As with regular meditation, begin by using your breathing to enter a state of relaxation. Similar to the previously discussed meditation ritual, visualize a natural place for your journey. This time, however, look for a hole in the ground or in a tree trunk and imagine it as an animal's den. This is where you'll enter and begin your descent toward the lower world. To vividly picture the downward journey, imagine yourself following the roots of a tree.

When you're ready, visualize yourself suddenly emerging from the ground and entering a vast, open space. Although this foreign place may look like the middle world of humanity, it will actually be the lower world. Imagine as many features and your own feelings as possible to make the place as real as you can in your mind. Observing the natural wonders of this place, you should eventually begin meeting animals. The first animal you see will rarely be your exact animal totem, but don't hesitate to ask. These other animals can also lead you to your guide.

Once you find the animal spirit that you're seeking, spend some time with it and get to know each other. Ask questions about the animal itself before moving on to asking for the answers that you came seeking. This is also where you can ask your animal spirit to take you on a quest around its realm and create whatever story you please. Shamanic drum recordings usually have different sections to guide your journey. Once it comes to the part featuring slow thumping, the journey should gradually come to a close as you return back to your realm.

Visualize yourself returning the same way you came, along the roots and through the tunnel, and only then allow yourself to emerge back in your room. Remember to make a journal entry that goes into the details of your journey, which will give you something to analyze and also help you make future journeys more intense and vivid as your mind gets used to the idea.

Bonding with Your Animal Totem

Strengthening your bond with your animal totem or spirit animal can and should be an ongoing effort that you can incorporate into your daily routine and spiritual practices. The simplest and most accessible method would be to study your preferred animal in as much detail as you can. This means turning a certain animal into a part of your life, particularly those of its qualities that you admire and draw inspiration from.

Learn as much as you can about the animal's habits, environment, innate traits, and instincts. The more you learn about the animal, the closer you'll feel to it, and you'll find that all of the animal's behaviors, characteristics, and way of life are full of powerful symbolism that you can relate to.

You can also take up various small rituals centered on honoring your animal totem. One way to do this is to build an altar in your animal's honor. Apart from fostering your creativity and providing some interesting decor in your home, an altar will serve as a place of reflection and meditation that you can use as a spiritual retreat. Your animal totem's altar will also be a place where you can give offerings to your power animal in the form of items and symbols that you associate with it. Symbolic items that represent a spirit animal can also be placed elsewhere throughout your home to ward off negative energy and symbolize your natural source of strength and inspiration.

Animal Dance and Movement

Last but not least, you can also strengthen the bond with your animal totem through your physical body. This is also a way for you to try and physically integrate some of the animal's power. It boils down to embodying the energy of your totem by adjusting your physical movements and stature to mimic the movements and natural positions of a certain animal. Of course, this doesn't mean walking around like an animal in your daily life. Rather, it's about assuming certain positions and making movements as part of some of your rituals, particularly when you're meditating or visualizing.

This can also be done during nature walks if you choose to meditate in nature as a way of getting even closer to animal guides and totems. Walking meditations, for instance, are powerful grounding rituals that are sure to make you more present in nature, which will also inevitably approximate you with animal spirits. The next chapter, which is all about nature spirits, will go into much more detail on connecting with nature on a spiritual level.

Chapter 5: Messages from Nature Spirits

For a lot of people, animals are the first association when nature is mentioned, but nature is home to many other spiritual entities. In some cultures, learning directly from nature is one of the central aspects of human life, and such ideas are deeply entrenched in their religious and spiritual practices. The harmony between nature and human beings is of great importance across cultures and civilizations, regardless of how much of their worship is focused explicitly on nature.

You can receive spiritual messages through nature as well.[14]

Because of their diversity, nature spirits are a somewhat broad term that describes a number of different spirit guides, entities, and concepts. Nature's wisdom is carried by spirits that inhabit trees, spiritual entities like fairies, the four elements of the natural world, and much more.

This chapter will provide you with some deeper insights into what nature spirits are, their types, how they influence the natural environment, and how they might be communicating with you. It will also feature a handful of practical exercises and tips that you can use to deepen your connection with nature, sharpening your eyes and ears to the things nature can tell you.

Understanding Nature Spirits

To start with, it's worth mentioning that many classifications will put animal spirits into the category of nature spirits, which is certainly where they belong. The reason why animal guides and spirits are often treated as practically separate is that animals themselves are incredibly diverse and have played such a prominent cultural role for many millennia. With that being said, nature spirits beyond animals are still quite diverse and numerous, covering many aspects of nature that you can see, feel, and imagine.

Apart from already mentioned spirits like those of trees and fairies, some of the other natural spirits that can be found scattered across spiritual traditions include gnomes, sylphs, nymphs, elves, mermaids, and many others. The number of these fantastical creatures seen as representing nature and her processes is matched only by the diversity of cultures and traditions that have observed and revered the natural world.

While the indigenous traditions of America are famous for their reverence of spirit animals and totems, there are also other ancient takes on nature worship that are fairly familiar to the modern Western world. Celtic traditions and various shamanic teachings elsewhere in the world have also left behind teachings and views on the reverence of nature that are studied and practiced to this day. In ancient Celtic culture, the people's relationship with nature was inseparably intertwined with spirituality.

The old Celts believed wholeheartedly in an entire world or realm of spirits existing in parallel with the physical world and being every bit as real, regardless of the limitations of human senses. The Celtic god

Cernunnos, for instance, was intimately associated with nature and regarded as the "lord of wild things." He was a god imbued with serenity, peace, and benevolence, portrayed visually as a human figure sporting a set of antlers and being surrounded by animals of various kinds. Being right with this deity was the way in which many ancient Celts sought to maintain harmony and balance with the natural world, with Cernunnos as an intermediary or incarnation of nature.

Perhaps more famously, the loosely defined traditions of shamanism are all about the natural world as something sacred, deeply spiritual, or even alive. According to various shamanic practices, spirits and spiritual energies permeate nature, and interacting with them through rituals and trances is a central aspect of human life. Shamans communicate with natural spirits on a deeper level, hoping to redirect their spiritual energies toward the benefit of human spirituality or health. In shamanism, virtually every aspect of nature is imbued with a living spirit, which includes animals, elements, plants, rivers, mountains, and other features observable to the human senses. Shamans might consider these features of nature to be living, spiritual beings in their own right, possessing consciousness and playing their roles in nature while also offering to teach wisdom to humans.

For the purposes of communicating with nature spirits, elemental spirits represent one of the most important categories. These spirits can be seen as embodiments of earth, air, water, and fire. Interpretations of such spiritual entities vary across traditions, but the four elements consistently play an important role in rituals aimed at spiritual and energy work. This is why rituals and altars in many esoteric practices usually feature some kind of symbolic representation for each of the elements.

The elements are seen as coming together to form the natural world, but each of the four is embodied by a set of spirits with unique properties and associations. This is why those who seek to communicate with elemental spirits might sometimes focus on the spirits connected to one or two elements instead of all at once. For instance, earth spirits tend to be associated with grounding and energetic stability, in addition to fertility and growth. Those looking to feel more centered in their direction while fostering a sense of stable grounding might seek the assistance of Earth spirits. These are usually the first spirits a practitioner will look for if their aim is to achieve a more intimate connection with the natural world.

Air spirits are all about movement and shifts, which often translates into matters related to energy and its flow in the natural world. These are highly communicative spirits who can provide a sense of clarity and stimulate the intellectual pursuits of the practitioner. They offer fresh perspectives on problems and situations in life, allowing people to analyze the details and find solutions through clarity of mind. On the other hand, the spirits of fire can be intense and inspire passion while representing transformation and fostering people's creativity. Communicating with fire spirits can invigorate you and increase your drive to achieve goals while increasing your vitality and readiness to effect change in your life.

Water elemental spirits are much calmer, having to do with your emotions and intuition. They also represent healing and flow in the broadest sense, with a penchant to interact with the deeper, subconscious recesses of your mind. If you're looking for inner wisdom or want to become better at processing your emotions, Water Spirits can provide tremendous guidance in that regard. All of these elemental spirits consistently influence the world in the realms of humans and spirits alike. Getting closer to these spirits entails deepening your relationship with nature on the most fundamental level since the elements themselves are nature's building blocks.

How Nature Spirits Communicate

The wisdom and inspiration in nature is found in all the little things you begin to notice once you become truly mindful, present, and grounded in a natural environment. These are things that most people normally don't notice because they are preoccupied with other pursuits as they go about their day. Listening to nature with every fiber of your being and being attentive to its finer processes on an intuitive level is the essence of communicating with nature spirits and heeding their guidance. This takes some effort, however, and it might even be considered a skill, but it's a skill that can be acquired quite easily.

Nature spirits are sure to communicate with you if you spend time outdoors and make an effort to listen to them. Channels of communication for these spirits can be incredibly diverse and will depend a lot on personal preferences. Essentially, any activity that you intuitively feel brings you closer to nature will enable you to communicate with its spirits. As is often the case with spiritual guidance, the insights and wisdom will come through the things you feel on the inside.

Nature spirits can also come to you at home, such as in your dreams or recurring symbols, signs, and feelings.[15]

Still, nature spirits will communicate in a lot of the ways that other spirit guides will. Any synchronicity that you observe when you're in nature can be highly meaningful and provide insights. Nature spirits can also come to you at home, such as in your dreams or recurring symbols, signs, and feelings. For instance, people will sometimes be consumed by visions of a particular place in the woods or elsewhere in the great outdoors, feeling inexplicably drawn to it. Such intuitive nudges should always be heeded and explored whenever the opportunity presents itself. You should also keep in mind the important role that animals and their spirits play in nature. Although animal guides are their own category, they will still sometimes interact with other nature spirits and participate in complex messages sent to you by nature.

Nature spirits can also make their presence known through all sorts of subtle or overt signs that seem only physical at first. Keep an eye out for abrupt changes in weather, feelings of a presence, or any kind of pattern you might notice in nature. The spirits will always be all around you when you enter an undisturbed natural location, but how, when, and if they're going to reach out to you directly can hardly be anticipated or preempted. The best thing to do is to just spend time within nature and open your mind and heart to its vibrations.

Hearing Nature Spirits More Clearly

To become more adept at listening to the messages that nature spirits offer, the most important thing you must do is strengthen your connection to nature. This doesn't just include seeking out specific nature spirits and guides. In a more general sense, you should find ways to become one with nature and immerse yourself in it in ways that too few people try these days. This means being physically and mentally present outdoors, spending time in nature, and engaging in various forms of meditation in environments that retain at least a moderate degree of their natural form.

Nature Walking Meditation

Engaging in meditation while taking a nature walk, also known as mindful walking, is a rather simple exercise. It's all about setting an intention to connect with nature or its spirits and doing your best to remain mentally and spiritually present while walking in a natural setting, ideally a forest. Make sure your steps are small and relaxed and that you're not rushing along the path. Keep your hands loose at your sides, and just let your body do its work automatically as you walk.

As usual, begin your meditation by focusing on your breathing and just observing it without thinking too much. A meditative walk in nature works best if you try not to think about and analyze your environment in any detail. This can be difficult because forests tend to overload the senses, but if you maintain focus on your breathing like you've learned to do, you'll get the hang of it. Continue observing your breathing and the way the air flows through you, energizing your body.

Once you're fully relaxed and walking spontaneously, slowly shift your focus to the way your feet interact with the soil beneath you. Maintain an awareness of this contact and gradually focus entirely on your steps, making sure to savor every sensation. Finally, you can begin to shift focus toward your environment by observing what you see, hear, and smell as impartially as possible. Use your senses as a new area of focus and when you're ready, try to visualize the nature spirits present in everything around you.

Nature Listening Meditation

The ambient sounds are one of the most stimulating aspects of a forest environment. This is why listening to nature can be so therapeutic and offers an excellent basis for meditation, especially with the goal of connecting to nature and hearing its spirits. It would work almost the same as a meditative nature walk, with the only difference being your focal point during meditation.

First, follow the same process until you arrive at a point where your focus shifts toward the environment and your actions during a walk. At that point, instead of focusing on the connection between your feet and the ground and all of your senses, set a narrower focus on the things you hear. Use your breathing as a focal point in case your mind begins to wander, and allow the sound of your breath to fuse with the ambient noises of the forest. Listen attentively and for as long as you can until you get a sharp picture of all the sounds around you, which will allow you to notice any sudden changes.

Any unusual sound, such as rustling or shifts in the wind, might carry messages from nature spirits if you listen closely enough. Don't hesitate to ask questions when paying attention to unusual noises, as you never know when an answer might come. You should also be on the lookout for any signs and symbols you might encounter, no matter how subtle. Keep your intention to hear nature spirits firmly in the back of your mind at all times.

Tree Spirit Meditation

Similarly, you can focus on specific nature spirits when you're out in the woods. Tree spirits are some of the most plentiful nature spirits in forested areas, so you can start there. It would work similarly to other forms of simple outdoor meditation, except that this time, you won't be walking. You should find a tree you feel drawn to, ideally one with a striking appearance and distinct characteristics. Meditation based on such a tree's spirit would work like most other meditations, but it would be based on the intention to connect with the tree's spirit.

Simply sit or stand close to the tree and enter a state of relaxation as you gradually begin visualizing the energy and spirits that permeate the tree from its roots and up to its branches. Focus on the idea that this tree is a living being like any other creature in the forest, with a powerful spirit coursing through it. Try to listen to the tree's sounds as the wind rustles its leaves or branches creak. Visualize a hidden world of thoughts and feelings within the tree and all of the things it would have witnessed over its long life. Open your mind and listen intently while also keeping an eye on your feelings, taking note of any sudden thoughts, sensations, or ideas that you might get.

Elemental Communication Ritual

Because the four basic elements of the world are such important aspects of nature, they're also a good channel of communication with nature spirits. Your elemental communication ritual can be anything you want it to be, with varying levels of complexity. You can indulge in elaborate rituals at an altar, using all sorts of esoteric materials to symbolize the elements, or you can simply seek to get closer to nature's elements by spending time with them outdoors.

For instance, sitting next to a river or a campfire is one of the best ways to meditate on the elements of water and fire. It will be much easier to visualize the spirit in things like rivers and crackling fires than it would be in a tree because of the obviously powerful energy that you can readily observe in these things. Similarly, you can observe the elemental spirits of air by listening to the endless cacophony of sounds that the wind produces, especially in the woods. Getting in touch with Elemental Earth is also easy if you walk barefoot.

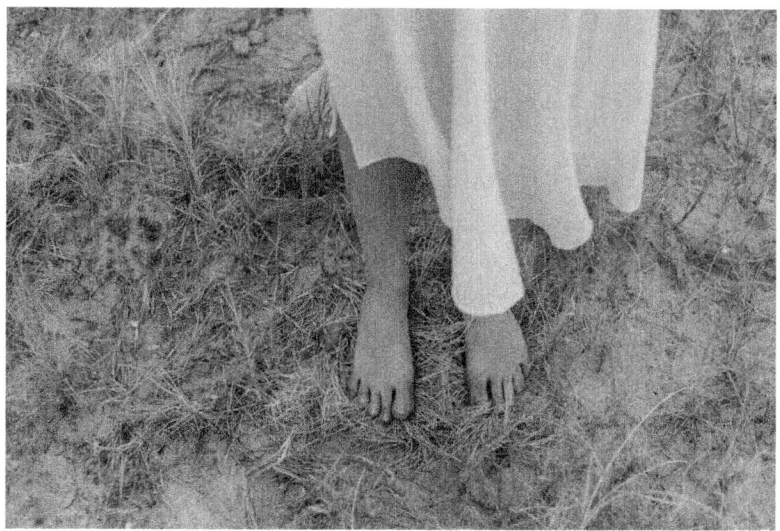

Connect to Earth by walking barefoot.[16]

In general, any day you spend out in nature can be turned into an elaborate elemental communication ritual if you focus on the right things. If you observe and listen to the elements like you've never done before, you'll uncover a whole new world that you've been missing. If you ask the right questions while at it, you might find just the answers you were looking for in a dash of wind, the rumbling of a river, or the lights and shadows cast by a dancing fire at a campsite.

Creating a Nature Spirit Altar

To get closer to nature and its spirits in your spiritual pursuits, you can also build a nature spirit altar in a similar way that you would with an animal spirit or animal totem. The similarity is in the intention behind the altar because its intention will be to honor a particular nature spirit that you're most interested in. As such, your altar should feature as many symbols of that specific nature spirit as possible. It can also be a more generalized altar for all your rituals related to nature, featuring natural objects like leaves, stones, moss, feathers, or anything else you find when you're out and about.

It's also a good idea to include symbols and other representations of mythical creatures or deities found in Native American culture, ancient Celtic religion, shamanism, or other spiritual systems focused on nature. The great thing about altars is that they're so modular and adaptable, so there will be a lot of room for you to put a personal spin on it. Items of personal value are always a welcome addition as well, especially if they're related to nature, your memories associated with nature, or an outdoor place that's especially meaningful for you. Remember to also include symbolic representations of the four elements, such as soil, candles, water, and anything that might symbolize air or the wind.

Moonlight and Fairy Communication

Summoning entities like fairies is an advanced visualization exercise, but with enough focus and a proper setting, you might be able to master the art through practice. It's important to take note of the associations that these entities have with aspects of the natural world to maximize your chances. Fairies, for instance, are commonly associated with moonlight, so the best time to try and communicate with them is during a full moon.

At a comfortable, quiet place outdoors, position yourself in a moonlit spot and establish a baseline meditative state for visualization. Use the energy of the white light showering down from the moon to visualize the light as a pathway to the realm of fairies. You can try to either visualize fairies or simply the hidden world that they inhabit. Ask questions and focus on any unusual sounds that stick out in your quiet nighttime surroundings. If you focus the power of your visualization, you might eventually hear a soft whisper or experience feelings of warmth and presence.

Chapter 6: Angel Signs and Communication

Although they don't take on physical forms in a way that animal guides or other nature spirits might do, angelic entities are among the most frequently contacted spirit guides. Angels or entities similar to them feature prominently in many religions despite their usual association with Christianity. As you've learned earlier, angelic spirit guides come in various forms and are often separated into two main groups, including personal guardian angels and those who ubiquitously wander different realms, contacting various people.

Angels and archangels, whether they are your guardians since birth or come into your life occasionally, can provide much comfort and reassurance. Their messages are supportive, wise, and inspiring. This chapter will teach you more about the various angelic entities in the spirit realm and how they might be communicating with you. You will also get insights into a few practical exercises and tips that will surely help you identify more signs and strengthen your bond with whatever angels are fluttering around in your life.

Angelic Beings and Their Roles

In the broadest sense, angels as a whole can be considered protective spiritual beings who also serve as divine messengers. Their very nature is all about guiding and protecting humanity and acting as a sort of intermediary between divinity and mortals. Although angels are usually associated with Christianity in the West, they don't necessarily have to be constrained to the teachings of a single religion. People from all religious backgrounds and even those who don't practice any faith can have a sense of something greater that exists above them and everyone else. Such people will also have a natural desire to get closer to that divinity, and that's where angels of all sorts come in.

Guardian angels and archangels, particularly the difference between the two, were already briefly discussed earlier in this book. Archangels, with their established and quite famous identities, have ubiquitous roles as sources of strength and inspiration for all of humanity. On the other hand, guardian angels cherish a more personal relationship with their humans, allowing for a lot more back-and-forth. This makes these angelic beings especially interesting in terms of spiritual communication.

The support you can get from your guardian angels is personalized and communicated through a lot of the usual spirit guide channels, such as dreams and synchronicities. A guardian angel might make his presence known when you're feeling discouraged and struggling with life's challenges. Apart from intuitively nudging you in the right direction or issuing warnings, guardian angels also provide an uplifting presence that can elevate your spirits and motivation. They're known to improve people's moods and promote optimism, which can be essential in keeping you on the right track.

Because of their connection with the divine and their residence in a much higher spiritual realm, angels can offer a unique perspective on problems and make you see things in a whole new light. Angels will also facilitate emotional, spiritual, and even physical healing in those who are struggling. Their presence is highly comforting and can help you overcome trauma and pain, similar to other spirit guides known for their supportive nature.

Your relationship with a guardian angel can be seen as an agreement or covenant that begins even before you are born into the physical world. Something else that sets guardian angels apart from other spirit guides is their detailed insight into your mind and soul, particularly your true goals and dreams. They understand your purpose and have access to information that's stored deeply in your heart. This profound personal understanding is why guardian angels are so supportive and encouraging.

Archangels can offer similar kinds of support, except with less of a personal touch. Archangels bring to the table a set of powerful spiritual associations and connotations, however, wielding immense divine power and possessing the ability to significantly affect the physical world. The most famous archangels include Raphael, Gabriel, Michael, and Uriel, among a few others. Respectively, they're represented by the colors yellow, blue, red, and green. In some traditions, these four archangels are also associated with the elements of air, water, fire, and earth, in the above order. In religious depictions, the archangels usually feature powerful tools or divine weapons that are specific to them, such as Michael's mighty sword, with which he slashes at injustice and malice.

Archangels also have certain specialties and roles, with Michael being known as a protector and a symbol of courage and divine truth. As such, Michael can protect you when you're feeling weak or offer guidance when you're lost. Raphael is a healer with an ability to inspire emotional and physical recovery in the afflicted. Gabriel is known as a communicative archangel who maintains a stable line with the divine and is usually called upon to facilitate communication with higher realms. Uriel is connected with the wilderness and its animals, guiding those who call upon him to a stronger connection with nature.

While communicating with a guardian angel is all about cherishing an existing relationship and strengthening your bond, archangels are usually directly invoked by name. This is done through rituals, prayer, meditation, and other methods, in addition to detecting and reading angelic signs that you might encounter in the world or in your mind and intuition. Your guardian angel is yours alone and will have a tailored approach to supporting you, while archangels are omnipresent and involved with all of humanity.

Common Angelic Signs

If you were born in a Christian cultural space, then you are probably very familiar with the concept of angels. Their role in the Christian religion has been intricately developed, and practicing the faith is, in many ways, an exercise in communicating with angels, especially archangels. Nonetheless, angelic entities should be seen as separate from individual religious dogmas, as their presence is universal and open to people from all backgrounds.

Before you learn about a few practical steps to increase your chances of receiving angelic messages, it's important to understand the wide range of signs that might signify their presence. Whatever kind of angelic entity you're interacting with, their presence can be felt or noticed through a variety of sensations or visual clues. Like a lot of other spirit guides, angels might announce their presence through scents, especially pleasant ones that smell sweet. Pay special attention to pleasant scents that emerge spontaneously without a clear source in your physical environment. For instance, a sudden scent of flowers is a common sign of angelic presence.

Because they often feature wings, angels might hint at their presence by leaving feathers in their wake. These can show up in various colors and sizes, especially in uncharacteristic places where birds don't usually visit. The more abnormal the place, the higher the likelihood is that there is an angel in your proximity. White feathers are the most frequently associated with angelic beings, although your personal guardian angel might sport a different color.

Angels are also known to communicate through numbers, especially repetitive and consecutive numbers that feel intuitively meaningful, such as 333, 777, 999, or a series of identical digits on a clock. If these numbers show up in your visual range at opportune times or recurrently, there is a good chance that an angel might be trying to draw your attention and tell you something. Angel numbers don't always have to be a succession of identical digits, however, and can include specific numbers that are personally meaningful to you, such as your birthday or that of a loved one.

There is a variety of interpretations of what various

Angel numbers.[17]

three-digit sequences of angelic numbers or peculiar clock digits might mean. You can try using established interpretations, but keep in mind that angels might not speak to every person in the same way. You are more likely to derive meaning from these numbers if you closely examine the context in which you see them, including location, synchronicities, your emotional state, and your present goals. For example, seeing 11:11 on a clock is often taken as a call from the spiritual realm, urging you to listen more attentively to spirit guides and focus on the big picture in your life. 12:12 is another essential clock number to watch out for, as it implies that you should tread beyond your comfort zone to achieve your goals. The three-digit sequences are usually interpreted to contain the following messages:

- **000** – Energy can affect outcomes in a lot that you do. This is why it's important to stay positive and goal-oriented instead of getting caught up on negativity from yourself or others.
- **111** – Your thoughts require your attention because of the profound ways in which they can impact your reality and determine outcomes.
- **222** – You are following the proper path toward your goals and should stay focused.
- **333** – This number is usually taken as a reminder that the angels, divinity, and other spirits are around you, guiding you along your path.
- **444** – A common sign of angelic presence, especially regarding your guardian angels who are giving you guidance.
- **555** – Symbolizes a wind of change in your life, according to divine will, but as a reminder that you should stay the course and not become complacent.
- **666** – Despite its bad rep, the number 666 is often an angelic sign carrying positive affirmations. It serves as a reminder that you must address your spiritual needs and strive for balance.
- **777** – A powerful numerical symbol confirming that you are following the right path and are striving decisively toward your goals and in accordance with divine will.
- **888** – Similarly to 555, this number symbolizes changes while also reminding you that you should embrace these shifts and seize the opportunities that they present.
- **999** – Referring to important changes in a broader sense, the number 999 reminds you of the changes within yourself, in addition to those around you. It implies that these changes should be welcomed and used to their full potential.

Stumbling upon a random coin can also signify an angelic presence in your life. Particularly important are any inscriptions, dates, and other details that the coin might contain, which can hold messages that only you can decipher within a specific personal context. You should also pay attention to sparks and other phenomena associated with light, especially during a ritual or meditation session. Tingling in the area of your crown chakra, temperature changes, warmth, tactile sensations, sudden joy, a pleasant breeze, reassuring voices, music, and much more can also imply the presence of an angel. Angels will also willingly use popular symbols regardless of what they actually look like, simply because these symbols are widely understood by people. Be on the lookout for angelic figures with wings, trumpets, swords, doves, chalices, or angelic wings.

Feeling the Angelic Touch

Since angelic spiritual entities are classified into different categories, communicating with them boils down to a set of various exercises, as well as goals for those exercises. Your journey toward forming a close relationship with the angels will also depend on your personal needs and circumstances. It might revolve around simply locating and reading their signs, but it can also rest on prayer, meditation, and simple spiritual bonding. The overarching goal is to become more sensitive to the angels and feel their presence in your life as clearly as possible. The exercises, rituals, and tips described below will offer a variety of avenues that you can take toward that end.

Connecting with Your Guardian Angel

Unlike some other spirit guides – such as those who emerge through animals – guardian angels will rarely show up in a form that you can observe with your eyes. Therefore, it's left to the eye of your mind, your intuition, and the power of your visualization to connect with your guardian angel if you want a face-to-face interaction. As with other spirit guides, however, the most important aspect of the connection will be in the things you intuitively feel and understand, so if you struggle with visualizing your guardian angel, you shouldn't give up.

Find or create a comfortable, soothing place that you can turn into your sacred space for meditating on your angelic connections. Try to make the spot personalized and symbolic with props and decorations. Lighting can also be very important when trying to communicate with angels, with soft, dim, soothing light being especially conducive to such communication. Fill your sacred space with pleasant scents as well, such as those of lavender or via smudging. The basis of the meditation will be similar to other such rituals discussed in the book thus far.

You can visualize a journey to a magical meeting place or envision a visitation from your guardian angel as he or she descends down to you and accompanies you in your meditation. Reflect on your soul's eternal bond with this guardian angel who has accompanied you since before birth and has faithfully observed all your trials and tribulations in life but also all your joyous moments. Try to mentally capture the entirety of what this long, personal relationship means, and you'll find it easier to achieve a sense of presence at any given moment. Using affirmations filled with gratitude can also be of great help.

Archangel Invocation Ritual

To invoke the archangels essentially means to summon them and call them into your presence. The simplest, traditional way of doing this is through prayer and religious worship. It can also be done through elaborate esoteric rituals with a pentagram or hexagram, conducted at an advanced altar that features four cardinal points, the elements, proper positioning, and much more. However, you don't have to be a master of esotericism to invoke an archangel and seek his guidance, and a lot of regular people do this every day with the four primary archangels.

You can also invoke angels through esoteric rituals with a pentagram.[18]

A simple invocation ritual rests upon intention, intuition, and powerful visualization. Begin with self-reassurance that the archangels are nearby and are ready to offer their guidance. First, turn east in the usual direction of Raphael and invoke him with a simple yet firm statement such as, "To my east, emerge Raphael." Use elements of Raphael's usual depictions to reinforce the visualization, such as his yellow robe, a powerful caduceus or staff in his hand, and the element of air. You can imagine him as a man-like figure with wings or as an incarnation of energy, as long as the shape and form are agreeable to your visualization skills.

For each of the other archangels, prepare a simple statement of invocation and say it aloud as you did with Raphael. As you continue facing east in your position, invoke Michael on your right-hand side, Gabriel behind you, and Uriel on your left. Remember their respective colors, and imagine each of them in connection with their respective tools and weapons, which include Michael's mighty sword, Gabriel's chalice, and Uriel's sheaf of wheat. Don't forget the elements they're associated with as well.

Visualizing all four of the archangels and convincing yourself that they're standing around you is a major exercise in visualization, which can take a lot of time and effort. Experiment with your setting, intentions, props, and altars as much as you need to until you create your perfect space that will facilitate such rituals. Once you're confident that you're visualizing the archangels, you can also use further verbal affirmations to address them directly after assembly.

Your intention and your reasons for invoking the archangels will depend on your needs as well, so if all you need is protection, then you can focus on invoking Michael alone. If you choose to use an altar, remember to set it facing east and assign four cardinal points for each archangel in the four corners of the altar. Every cardinal point should also feature an elemental symbol, and your invocation rituals will benefit from prayers and the ritualistic use of candles. Every archangel can also have their individual candle in their respective color.

Journaling Angel Signs

The signs discussed earlier can show up seemingly at random or during one of your deliberate attempts to contact the angels. Whether the sign was a response to your inquiry or a prompt from an angel trying to initiate contact has no implications as to the sign's relevance.

They're all equally important, and you should make an effort to record every association, synchronicity, or symbol, no matter how subtle or random they might seem.

Angels come in many shapes, and they're one of the most widespread kinds of spirit guides making their way around humans. Because of this ubiquitous presence and the sheer diversity of their signs, it's a good idea to have a separate ledger serving as a journal used exclusively for angelic signs.

Write what you hear and feel and draw what you see, even if you completely forget about it within the hour. You never know when you might see something else that reminds you of a sign you saw previously, and a sudden realization of clarity just clicks. Some signs will only make sense when compared to previous experiences, which will give them a full context. Your angel sign journal is something you'll continuously study and reference as you try to understand more about what archangels and guardian angels are trying to tell you.

Angel Card Reading

Angel oracle cards are another mode of communication you might consider when trying to receive hints from angels or archangels. Angel cards are rather popular, so your first step is to pick a deck that you find most appealing. This is the part where your intuition will play an essential role. Once you pick the perfect deck of angel cards, you'll be able to use them in many ways and for various questions and messages, similar to how you'd use animal oracle cards.

Your deck can be as simple as containing yes and no answers to questions, or it can be rather complex, in which case it'll likely come with some sort of manual or guidebook for detailed interpretation. In either case, the important thing is to set clear intentions and prepare the right questions before using your cards. For simple questions that are satisfied with simple answers, you can use a simple one-card spread for a quick inquiry. Shuffle your deck thoroughly and ask a question or make a request before drawing a card to receive an answer. You can ask your questions internally, but it's also a good idea to verbalize them or even use short prayers and affirmations as if you were invoking an archangel.

Apart from a three-card spread that provides an answer with bonus insights about your past and future, just like with animal cards, you can also try a five-card spread. This spread is the perfect middle ground between simple answers and complex readings, as it can provide more information and insights regarding potential paths, propositions, and tough decisions. All you have to do is ask for guidance regarding your problem, pull five cards, and arrange them in the shape of a cross with one card in the middle and the other four on each side of it.

The central card will provide the most generalized response to your inquiry. Respectively, the cards on its left and right will refer to the past as it influences the current situation and a potential future outcome, just like in a three-card spread. The cards on the bottom and top of the central card will provide insights into your reasons for asking the question and any potential changes or opportunities that might arise from your situation.

Depending on the kind of deck you acquire, your cards might also be suitable for seven-card, Celtic cross, heart-shaped spreads, and much more. You'll also find that most decks allow for a lot of experimentation so that you can adjust them to your communication rituals in a way that best suits you and your needs.

Chapter 7: Reconnecting with Departed Loved Ones and Ancestors

For a lot of people, the main interest they have in spiritual communication is the prospect of making contact with loved ones who are no longer with them. Another common hope that spiritually curious people throughout history have had is to strengthen their bond with their ancestors and heritage. As such, departed loved ones and ancestors are some of the most important spirit guides.

Both of these kinds of spirit guides can be sources of immense strength. Getting in touch with them has the potential to make an individual feel held while also providing a powerful sense of belonging. Most human civilizations have always attributed great importance to ancestors as a means of positioning the living generation within a continuum that stretches beyond a human lifetime. On the other hand, people from across the world have always had to contend with the grief of losing the people they held dear, with many different approaches to processing these feelings.

Spiritual communication allows you to communicate with departed loved ones.[19]

Whether it's about ancestors or departed loved ones, the central theme is always the human desire to converse with those who are no longer physically present. Some people want to do this as a way of strengthening their roots, while others are looking for closure after a loss, but whatever the motive might be, this kind of spiritual communication is all about spiritual balance and comfort. This chapter will teach you more about the spirit guides found in these categories while also going over a few practical exercises that will help you get in touch with those who are no longer with you.

Departed Loved Ones, Ancestors, and the Nature of Their Communication

Why connecting with ancestors and loved ones who have passed has been so important in innumerable cultures is a multifaceted question. Part of it has to do with the fact that people across time and space have always had many things in common, particularly in regard to concerns and experiences in their lives on Earth.

Existential questions, life's trials and tribulations, and spiritual exploration are universal aspects of life that all human beings share.

To tackle such challenges, especially with respect to things that are yet to come, people have always looked for help and guidance from those who have experience in these domains. As such, the experience and legacy of those who have lived out their entire lives and seen the end have always naturally come into focus.

Departed loved ones and ancestors have not only had the full experience of life, but they also share much more with their descendants than with other, more distant people. This is what makes such spirits an eternal object of fascination and searching for people in need of guidance and spiritual support.

When you need someone who's been through the same things you're currently going through and also comes from the same place or even the same home as you, your ancestors and departed loved ones will provide the strength, inspiration, and wisdom that you need.

In a spiritual sense, ancestors and loved ones are spiritual entities that dwell in the realm of spirits while still retaining an interest in communicating what wisdom and insights they can to those who've come after them and are still among the living. The spirits of some people who have passed might not always have such interests, choosing instead to focus fully on the matters of beyond. However, it's exceedingly rare that the spirit of someone you were close with will have no desire to communicate with you on at least a basic level. Sometimes, they'll merely make their presence known without saying much that's concrete, and you will find that this is enough.

The personal nature of the bond and the aforementioned common ground that you'll have with these spirit guides will make this relationship feel like a true companionship. Knowing that others have gone through the challenges that you're facing, prevailed, and are now watching over you as you move through the motions will - at the very least -make you feel less alone in any hardship. This is the essential nature of communicating with your ancestors and departed loved ones.

Apart from enriching your life with their comforting presence, these spirit guides will certainly give you intuitive nudges and subtly point you toward decisions and paths at times. To that end, they might communicate through reminders, flashbacks, and other sudden bursts of clarity that occur at opportune times. The overwhelming sense that a loved one or an ancestor is happy with the path you are taking and is proverbially smiling down upon you is an experience that many people will have in their lives. This is one of the clearest signs of a benevolent spiritual presence by an entity that knows you intimately and understands what you're going through.

Common Signs of Ancestral or Departed Presence

Keeping in touch with departed loved ones and ancestors is one of the most intuitive forms of spiritual communication. In part, this is because of the deeply personal, emotional, and spiritual threads that bind an individual to these spirits in a way that doesn't exist with most other entities. Beyond overt signs and information, to communicate with these spirit guides is to feel the warmth and comfort of their support. For many people, this relationship boils down to feeling and cherishing the sense that these spirits are present in their lives more than engaging in informational back-and-forth.

Your ancestors or loved ones who have passed can communicate with you in two main ways. Firstly, this communication might be a one-time sign, such as a single dream or vision. Having a dream about someone who has recently passed away is a common way in which this happens for many people. By visiting you in a dream shortly after their departure, a loved one might be trying to help you process the heavy emotional residue of your loss. The dream may or may not be pleasant, but this is almost always a way for a loved one to help you adjust to the new reality of living without them while giving you some initial closure. For most people, the grieving process extends well beyond a single dream, of course, but this simple visitation is an important early step.

On the other hand, these guides can also communicate with you on an ongoing basis. How frequently that communication will occur depends both on the spirit's intentions and your own efforts. If you actively cherish the connection and engage in rituals to deepen the relationship, the frequency of the messages will undoubtedly increase. Prolonged communication with a departed loved one can last throughout a period of grieving or other personal struggle, but it can also be a life-long interaction. With ancestors, the emphasis is especially strong on long-term exchanges with the spirit realm because this relationship tends to be more meditative, ritualistic, and infused into lifelong spiritual and religious practice.

The spiritual energy that comes through from your ancestors will manifest and strengthen through your efforts to explore and approximate your heritage and your place in that long chain. As such, it's a more proactive search for signs and clues that increase in frequency as your curiosity grows. Departed loved ones tend to be a lot more spontaneous and free-flowing with the messages they send. Apart from dreams, they might also manifest through scents, songs, tastes, or images that irresistibly remind you of that person.

These clues will show up as synchronicities at meaningful moments and steer your mind and feelings in certain directions via your intuition. The signs that departed loved ones will send your way can be immeasurably diverse and subject to all manner of personal variations. There is no golden universal formula in relationships this personal, so a lot of these signs will only be known and identifiable when seen by your eyes and experienced through your emotions. The important thing is to cherish the memory of the person who was close to your heart with as much detail as possible, and then it will be easy for you to notice when they are trying to communicate in ways that only you can truly understand.

Receiving Messages from Those Who Have Passed On

As in the case of angels and archangels, departed loved ones and ancestors have similarities, but they are categories with defined differences. Increasing the presence of either in your life is once again a deeply personal journey that you are encouraged to modify, adapt, and adjust so that you are meeting your specific spiritual needs as best you can. Not everyone who seeks to connect with a departed loved one will be dealing with the trauma of an unresolved loss while seeking closure and emotional catharsis.

On the contrary, people who are at perfect peace with the natural passing of someone they hold dear can have a wide range of reasons to want to explore a deeper relationship with their loved one's spirit. Keep these personal preferences and differences in mind when learning about the following exercises, as they can benefit immensely from your personal input and adjustments.

Creating a Memory Altar

A memory altar can be an incredibly powerful tool that'll help you channel energy between yourself and a departed loved one – *or even your entire ancestral lineage.* It would work similarly to any other altar dedicated to a specific kind of spirit guide and can be as simple or as complex as you want it to be. The important thing is that your memory altar features as many items associated with the people you're remembering as possible.

Consider creating a memory altar.[20]

These objects can be photographs, heirlooms, other personal items, or anything else that once belonged to a person or is a strong reminder of them. The idea is for these reminders to maintain your focus on the memories of a person while you're at the altar performing a ritual or meditating. Personal items will be the defining feature, but your altar can still feature other default characteristics of an altar, such as religious décor and things symbolizing the four elements.

Your memory altar will serve as a spiritual retreat in a quiet place and a location where you can symbolically meet your departed loved ones and ancestors. It provides a special place where you can visualize convening with these spirits, asking them questions, and seeking their guidance. It'll also be a place for honoring these people and giving offerings to them.

Ancestral Meditation

As usual, meditation will serve as one of the methods of communication with these spirit guides. If you build a memory altar, you'll have an easily accessible place for this kind of meditation in your home, filled with all sorts of props that will potentiate the flow of energies and keep your intention strong. To create a setting conducive to this kind of communication, you can also use music that the departed once enjoyed or something that's associated with your ancestors as a whole. As a general rule, meditation works best in silence, but in this case, a melody can strengthen a sense of presence and familiarity while also triggering certain emotions. As long as the music is at a low volume and is relaxing, it's something worth experimenting with.

Begin by getting into a comfortable position and a breathing exercise for relaxation. Position yourself at your memory altar or surround yourself with meaningful items that remind you of the people you are trying to communicate with. You can visualize that the departed is at your home and is present in the room with you, or you can imagine a more complex encounter scenario happening at another place, particularly a location that's attached to shared memories. You can also picture a gathering of supportive ancestors sitting around a table or, better yet, your altar. Create a meditative journey similar to how you would meet your power animal or a nature spirit and gradually work your way toward the moment when you can ask questions and seek guidance. Make sure to make a written note of any feelings and insights once you're done with your meditation.

Letter to a Departed Loved One

Sometimes, the best approach is to simply engage in direct conversation with the spirit of a departed loved one. Apart from being direct, this form of dialogue is subtle, personal, and easy to engage in wherever you find yourself. You can write this letter when you're spending time out in nature or at home. The only thing that matters are the contents of the letter, which should feature plenty of back-and-forth and treat your departed loved one as much as a living person as possible. Don't simply ask questions and make demands. Try to make it a real conversation, providing family updates, comments, and reminiscing that your loved one would be interested in.

While you can write this private letter anywhere, it matters where you place it after you're done. It should be left at a meaningful place where the presence of the departed is felt the strongest. You'll have the best idea of what place evokes these emotions in you, but some of the usual examples include the person's resting place at the cemetery, shared favorite locations, locations of important past events between you and the departed, or a memory altar. It's also a good idea to read the letter aloud at your memory altar to verbalize the message and strengthen the connection. You can keep this letter and read it as an overture to meditation and visualization, using it as a starting point that commences a conversation.

Automatic Writing

Because parts of your departed loved ones and ancestors live on inside you, you'll have a natural advantage when it comes to mediumship with these spirits. You are bound to have quite a few things in common with them in terms of your personality, mentality, and intuitive feelings. This is why automatic writing can be a very fruitful addition to your efforts of channeling messages between yourself and these spirits. As described earlier in the book, automatic writing allows you to pour out the thoughts and emotions that come to you via intuition without any filters, unclouded by analysis and second-guessing.

Refer back to the basics of automatic writing as discussed in the third chapter) and think of the best way to direct this method at your departed loved one or ancestors. The aforementioned letter, for instance, is an excellent opportunity to use automatic writing. The spirit might already be active around you and trying to communicate, so if you use automatic writing for your letter, you might find that the writing becomes a joint exercise between you and the spirit. You never know what the spirit might channel through you as you write, so it's important to spend some time analyzing the content later on. Their messages could be coded, subtle, and difficult to spot at first, being hidden in plain sight and appearing as your own words at first glance.

Dream Journaling

Every dream that references your ancestors or departed loved ones in any way will be extremely meaningful, no matter how simple or shallow it might seem at first glance. It's important to keep a clear record of these dreams, featuring as much detail as possible. Write down the details of conversations, any symbols you see, or any feelings you experience in the dream. All of these will contain essential insights that you must analyze to derive their full meaning.

Keeping a dream journal can strengthen your connection with your departed loved ones.[21]

It can also help if you practice setting intentions before going to sleep, especially during the last few minutes before you go under. Focus your mental energy and try to imagine a dream with as much detail as possible and let yourself shut down right in the middle of your thought process. Even if this doesn't produce the exact dream you were hoping for, it's very likely to make your dream more vivid and memorable. Keeping a dream journal is also known to train the brain's ability to recall dreams after waking up. This might eventually unlock lucid dreaming as well, in which you'll control the narrative and have any conversation you desire. Dreams are best remembered right after you awake, so your journal and a pen should be kept handy on your nightstand so that you can start writing first thing in the morning.

Chapter 8: Communicating with Ascended Masters

On a plane of existence much higher than that of regular humans and perhaps even that of other spirit guides, there exist figures commonly referred to as the ascended masters. According to most interpretations, these are enlightened beings that occupy a higher dimension and have transcended beyond the processes described in major religions, such as the cycle of reincarnation. Usually, they were once people who had ascended to this higher plane by elevating their consciousness and spirit.

The ascended masters are usually given a few unique properties that separate them from the spirit guides discussed

Ascended masters are enlightened beings that occupy a higher dimension.[22]

thus far. They are still there to offer guidance and wisdom to people, but their realm is on a whole other level. The ascended masters can be seen as the highest echelon of guiding spiritual entities, but that doesn't mean they are beyond reach. Their power is in the immortal example they have set for other spiritually-minded people who came after them.

Seasoned mediums or those practitioners who put enough effort and practice into spiritual communication can learn how to receive messages even from the highest order of spiritual beings. This final chapter will close off the story about spiritual communication by teaching you more about these special kinds of spirit guides. You'll also learn how you might be able to absorb some of the wisdom that they can teach if you're willing to go the extra mile.

Who Are the Ascended Masters?

Generally speaking, the ascended masters represent spiritual teachers who have elevated themselves to levels of spirituality and consciousness beyond normal human comprehension. Embodied and exemplified by spiritual giants and deities such as Christ, Gautama Buddha, Mary, Guanyin, St. Germain, and others, the ascended masters often feature rather human forms or are outright based on people who once lived.

The concept of ascended masters is a major theme in the traditions of theosophy, which is a mixture of religious practices and philosophy that originated in the 19th-century United States. Theosophy is often not proclaimed to be a religion, but at the very least, it can be seen as a philosophical and spiritual system that brings together religious and philosophical teachings from across the world. It prominently features aspects of Eastern religions like Hinduism and Buddhism, as well as ancient European philosophy. Since the early days of theosophy, the ideas surrounding the ascended masters have proliferated and been adopted into various other practices as well.

According to theosophical tradition, the ascended masters are defined by having past human incarnations. As such, they were once ordinary people who, through tremendous spiritual work and effort, were able to complete a number of transformations. These transformations, also referred to in theosophy as initiations, allowed the ascended masters to reach such a level of spiritual enlightenment that they eventually escaped the cycle of rebirth. It is the hope of those who seek to contact and follow the example of the ascended masters that they'll be able to draw at least some of that wisdom and power to be used toward their own spiritual development. This is why the ascended masters, beyond strict theosophical practice, are often regarded as another group of spirit guides.

Although these enlightened souls now dwell in realms beyond the five human senses, the mark that they left upon the world was tremendous. Their legacy is one of wisdom, passion, healing, enlightenment, and compassion. In many cases, the ascended masters helped others both spiritually and physically during their time on earth, as opposed to simply pursuing their own enlightenment.

One of the defining features of the ascended masters is their universality across different cultures. This body of teachings draws from all major religious traditions and brings them together into one comprehensive spiritual system. They bring together cultures, races, ethnicities, and religions, representing a wealth of spiritual heritage and wisdom. It's also not uncommon for some of the ascended masters to be venerated in multiple major religions – with one example being Jesus, who plays a prominent role in both Christianity and Islam.

Free from the cycle of rebirth as understood in Eastern traditions and of worldly suffering, the ascended masters have attained immortality through their spiritual perfection. Unlike guardian angels and other spiritual entities that might follow you on your path, the ascended masters can be understood as healers, prophets, and teachers, each representing a unique individual with their own characteristics.

One of the essential truths that follow from the human past behind every ascended master is that every person has the capacity to become one. Ascending to this level of spirituality and higher consciousness is an exceedingly rare, historic anomaly, of course, but it's an ideal that all spiritually curious individuals can strive toward.

The Value and Ways of Ascended Master Communication

Perhaps the greatest source of power and meaning of the ascended masters is in the shining examples that they've set for humanity. As such, these unique guides can provide people with inspiration and serve as sources of strength in your time of need. Every ascended master is also a fountain of learning, offering profound insight into life paths that lead toward spiritual actualization.

Listening to what the ascended masters can teach will guide you on a path toward self-empowerment, spiritual and emotional healing, enlightenment, and much more. While other kinds of spirit guides can offer similar guidance, the ascended masters represent unique stories of spiritual life that can teach you a lot about the often difficult yet incredibly fruitful ways of living that these historical figures once lived. Developing a close relationship with one or more of the ascended masters is akin to finding a mentor on your spiritual journey, which is a role that's markedly different from that of most other spirit guides.

Another way in which the ascended masters differ from other spirit guides is in how their presence is felt. Whereas other spirit guides might make themselves known through symbols, messages, and visions, the ascended masters are more likely to be intuitively felt. Common signs of connection with an ascended master include feelings of profound inner peace, sudden clarity regarding the right path in a difficult time in your life, and overall feelings of love and compassion.

A regular spirit guide will speak to you as directly as they can, often about a specific issue that's troubling you. They'll also spontaneously leave messages that will await your discovery and interpretation. On the other hand, communicating with the ascended masters will often be a proactive endeavor on your part. They might sometimes come into your life when they are needed, but mostly, it's up to you to seek out the guidance of the ascended masters and build your personal relationship with them.

An ascended master will communicate with you when you put in the effort to contact them because you'll feel their presence on an emotional and spiritual level. They will communicate with those individuals who follow a spiritual path toward enlightenment with tremendous dedication. An ascended master's central role is to help human beings along that path and guide them toward higher levels of consciousness, with the hope that a gifted few might ascend through their initiations and reach the same level.

That spiritual support is the primary benefit of building a connection with the ascended masters. While other spirit guides will empower you with specific insights and messages of a deeply personal nature, the ascended masters are there to imbue your spirit with strength, clarity, and inspiration. They will bring compassion and love into your life, reinforcing your sense that you aren't alone and that there's a spiritual ideal that's worth striving for.

Getting in Touch with Ascended Masters

There are many ways in which you can foster a relationship with one or more ascended masters. Since a lot of them are central figures in major religions, practicing these faiths can also be seen as a way of cherishing your relationship with an ascended master. However, mainline religions maintain interpretations that are fairly different from those found in the traditions of theosophy. As such, trying to get in touch with the ascended masters on your own can be seen as a complementary endeavor that can enhance your conventional religious practices.

Meditation, daily rituals, and other similar activities can only serve to propel you further on your path toward spiritual fulfillment, as you'll find in the instructions discussed below.

You can get in touch with ascended masters through meditation.[23]

Meeting Ascended Masters through Visualization and Meditation

Since the ascended masters are well-defined individuals with their own personalities, trying to connect with them directly will work very well as a meeting visualization. Refer back to what you've learned earlier about shamanic journeying or meeting your animal totem in an envisioned place of wonder and natural spirituality. Try to come up with a similar scenario that fits particularly well with the ascended master you're trying to visualize. Think of creating a story such as a meeting with

Christ in Nazareth or a walk along the Ganges in ancient India with Siddhartha before he attained Buddhahood.

Imagine a peaceful plane in a higher-dimensional space where insightful meetings can occur between the curious souls of mortals and those of the ascended masters. Set your intention toward a particular ascended master, a place, and a question before you begin your meditation. Focus your mind's eye upward toward a plane of existence that exists as physically higher than the observable world of humans. Follow a visualized stairway upward as it's conjured up from white light or the moonlight on a clear night.

Whatever kind of place you picture in your mind and whatever way you imagine will lead you there, focus on the ascended master and all of his unique characteristics. Famous and legendary figures have a whole lot that defines them, so it should be easier to imagine them as real beings with faces and traits. This is why it's important to understand the ascended masters who pique your interest and study them a fair amount before thinking you are ready to meet them. When the interaction finally comes, make sure that you know what you want to ask and are prepared to receive the answers.

Daily Wisdom Practice

Your relationship with the ascended masters is something that you can work on every day. There are many ascended masters residing on those higher planes of existence beyond the ones briefly mentioned earlier. Practicing the wisdom of the ascended masters on a daily basis can work as a daily meditation plan in which every day of the week is dedicated to a particular master. You can start the week by meditating upon the life and works of Christ on Monday, and Siddhartha Gautama on Tuesday, before taking a stroll into ancient Chinese spirituality or Hinduism on the following day.

How you practice wisdom and interact with the ascended masters on a daily basis is entirely up to you. The only true rule that you must heed is the necessity of studying these figures and their legacy as much as you have the time for. For instance, a simple yet potentially profound way to start your morning is to find a quote by a particular ascended master and spend some time reflecting on what it means. Many of the ascended masters have left behind a wealth of earthly wisdom, which is studied by billions of people to this day.

Their quotes and tidbits of their expansive minds often hold a lot more meaning than is immediately apparent. If you spend at least fifteen minutes during your morning routine analyzing such thoughts and meditating on their meaning, you might eventually discover that you're starting to look at certain things in a new light. Every time you meditate upon one of the masters, remember that the main goal is to bring at least a bit of influence and inspiration from them into your life. You must set clear intentions toward that end, with an understanding that their presence alone can give you an immense spiritual boost even if you don't engage in any concrete back-and-forth.

Sacred Reading and Reflection

In a way, you can choose your preferred ascended master and develop your bond with them similarly to how you would with your animal totem. This similarity concerns the part of animal totem bonding that has to do with studying the animal you feel drawn toward.

Remember: many of the ascended masters used to be humans who achieved their high status through intense spiritual work, thus leaving a mark on major world religions. These faiths all feature an immense body of scripture, sacred texts, and endless other material that you can study. Studying these texts or just learning about the stories from an ascended master's mortal life are both great ways of making yourself feel closer to such figures.

Your first impression might be that it's going to be difficult to relate to the struggles of people who lived 2,000 years ago or even earlier. Once you start reading, however, you'll find that there is a whole lot about the human experience that hasn't really changed on a fundamental level. This is especially true of spiritual pursuits and existential questions, which remain as relevant as ever and essentially the same. Some of the Hindu Vedas, for example, go back more than 3,000 years, and having such direct insight into the spirituality of those days can be a fascinating experience.

It's important that you never read these sacred texts merely as a way to kill time or as a fashion statement. These writings demand attention and should be read mindfully, regardless of your cultural background or personal beliefs. If you truly commit to studying sacred texts and scripture, it's a good idea to start a separate journal where you can make quick notes of your observations, interpretations, and feelings about the things you read.

Appendix: Spirit Messages – Common Signs and Symbols

Now that you understand how spiritual communication works and what the usual sources of these messages are, it's up to you to come up with routines and ritual combinations that best fit into your lifestyle and interests. Keep in mind that honing your intuition and becoming more present and aware in your daily life is the key to noticing spirit messages.

To round things off, this appendix will provide a small but handy glossary of common messages, signs, and symbols that you're likely to encounter when searching for communications from your spirit guides. The appendix will also serve as a partial recap by summarizing some of the messages already discussed in the previous chapters and combining them with a few that weren't mentioned. Having all of these listed out and briefly summarized in one place will hopefully allow you to keep the list close at hand for quick reference both in your daily life and your rituals.

Animals

Since animals can be such important conduits of spiritual communication, they deserve special attention. Be on the lookout for any animals that you feel a special connection to, and take note of their powerful symbolism that can be found in almost all spiritual traditions in history. When an animal crosses your path, pay heed to how it behaves, what it does, and where the encounter occurred. If a wild animal stops to look at you and gives you attention, especially in a natural setting, you might be witnessing a powerful sign.

Birds

While birds fall under the broader category of animals, some species are particularly noteworthy. Refer to earlier parts in this book that mention many important symbols associated with animals, which have cropped up in many of the world's religions. The behavior of birds can be especially meaningful, particularly if they land on or near you and display an uncharacteristic inclination toward interacting with you.

Butterflies

Butterflies are a common symbol of transformation, owing to the natural way in which they develop and enter the world. Some traditions consider them to symbolize benevolent souls coming to visit you. Turn to your introspection and intuition, paying attention to the person or memory that seems to come to your mind most frequently when you encounter a butterfly. As such, a butterfly can represent the fact that a departed loved one has successfully made it over to the other side or is sending you a message of love and support.

Celestial Bodies

The stars, moon, and sun can all carry important messages if you know what to look for. Noticing patterns in the night sky or around the rising or setting sun as it casts its light through the clouds around it can convey meaning depending on how you're feeling or what you're thinking at that moment. The same holds true for the moon and its many shapes, locations, and colors, ranging from red to silver.

Clock Signs

Clocks, and time in general, can sometimes elicit strange feelings, especially when your mind starts noticing patterns and synchronicities. If you observe a perfect set of identical numbers, such as 22:22 or 11:11, or a symmetrical instance like 13:13, it could be a message from a spiritual source. Perhaps a person you hold dear is thinking of you, or it could be a departed loved one or another form of spirit guide. In a time of struggle, this realization can offer reassurance and support. At times of happiness or success, it could mean that someone who passed away is looking over you and sharing in your joy.

Cloud Patterns and Shapes

Similarly to celestial bodies, clouds should be observed whenever you have the opportunity to spend some time in reflection and introspection. Look for patterns and shapes that might materialize as the clouds slowly rumble along their way across the sky, and you might be surprised by what you find. Due to their immense variability in size and shape (and their constant shifting), clouds usually abound in meaning and are a common channel that spiritual entities use to communicate. Reading into clouds can also have therapeutic effects and can be incorporated into various meditative exercises.

Coins

A coin is another one of those ubiquitous small objects that can show up in odd places and at peculiar times. It's not merely due to their association with money and wealth that coins have often been associated with luck when found lying around. If you run into a coin when you least expect it, you should take note of the situation in which you found it and look at potential synchronicities. Inspect such a coin closely, and you might be surprised by the numbers or words on it and how they might relate to your latest thoughts, intentions, or actions.

Displacement of Objects

As you've learned, various inanimate objects can serve as conduits of spiritual messages. In particular, if you find that certain items disappear, move, or reappear inexplicably, it could be a spiritual entity's way of trying to communicate. You should be mindful of how some objects – particularly ones that you thought you had lost – reappear at times and places that seem oddly coincidental. An object might reappear exactly when you need it, which is clear enough, but it might also show up only for you to then realize that you need it.

Feathers

While feathers were discussed earlier as one of the common signs of spiritual communication, it's also worth noting that they are widespread in the physical world. Not every feather will carry a special meaning or message for you, especially if you can find a clear, logical explanation for its presence at a certain place. As always, look for synchronicities and try to determine if a feather has shown up within a meaningful concept. Finding a feather next to a bird nest and having one flutter on a dash of wind through your window and land directly on you are two very different scenarios.

General Repetition

Repetition and patterns, in the broadest sense, are major signs of spiritual messaging reaching you from beyond. Pattern recognition is an innate human ability, so don't let yourself succumb to confirmation bias, but also keep in mind that certain things will undoubtedly repeat and reoccur for a reason. If you notice certain colors, numbers, or codes consistently showing up, especially within a context that also seems to repeat itself, it's a good idea to give it more thought and analysis.

Light Disturbances

The flickering of lights or similar malfunctions is often misconstrued as a sign of paranormal activity, but this is a pop-culture misconception. Remember what you learned about energy and the important role it plays in the universe, your life, and all things spiritual. All of the spiritual entities you might be communicating with can, in essence, be seen as forms of energy, not too different from electricity. If a light flickers and signifies a spiritual presence, this will be a time for listening and observing, not worrying.

Moments of Clarity

Having a moment of clarity is not an uncommon consequence of spiritual intervention. It can be a spirit guide's way of telling you that you have reached an important realization or are about to uncover a great truth that will have a significant effect on your life. If you find yourself arriving at an important conclusion suddenly and without a clear, logical path in your thinking, you can be fairly certain that this important information was communicated to you by an overseeing spiritual force.

Music

As an essential aspect of the human experience, music carries a lot of meaning and energy, operating on various frequencies. The human mind has a special keenness for music and has a way of attaching memories, experiences, places, people, and much more to specific songs. As such, music lends itself to all manner of synchronicities that can make you feel and remember many things. Look for coincidences, such as a certain song coming on at a special moment that relates to it in your memories and thoughts. For instance, thinking of a departed loved one while switching on the radio, only to find that it's playing their favorite song, is a powerful message.

Orbs

Orbs, particularly those showing up in photographs, look like light balls that hover around people, objects, and spaces in some photos. Mediums commonly interpret these as signs of a spiritual presence. They usually don't carry a lot of specific meaning and are instead just a way for spirit guides to make their presence known. Still, the meaning of these orbs can vary depending on the context. If your photograph depicts an important event in your life, such as a wedding, then the presence of benevolent spiritual entities can serve as a source of reassurance.

Recurrent Waking

Waking too often in the middle of the night is usually a sign of sleep problems, but if it takes on a strange pattern, it might be much more meaningful and positive than a health issue. If, for instance, you find yourself frequently waking up at the same time, it may well be an attempt by a spiritual entity to bring your attention to something. Such a pattern of waking might also be accompanied by a recurrent thought or feeling that always follows, all of which can have a personal meaning for you.

Scents

Your sense of smell can uncover a strange presence, send you on a rollercoaster of memories, or provoke any number of intense reactions. Thanks to relational memory, certain smells can become attached to past events, feelings, and especially people. Many people have had the peculiar experience of noticing a smell that seems identical to that of a person they know well. If that person happens to be a departed loved one, noticing such a smell can be a powerful experience that reinforces their presence in spirit.

Sensations

Physical sensations can mean a lot of different things, but it's not uncommon for them to be caused by spiritual messages. The idea of being "touched" frequently appears in discussions of spiritual experiences because of this. Tactile feelings that have no clear origin in anything physical and when no contact is made with a person or object can be a strong indication of a spiritual presence. If you happen upon such an experience, take note of the context in which it occurs. If it coincides with a spiritual communication ritual or thoughts of a departed loved one, any physical sensation can become one of the most powerful spiritual messages you'll ever experience.

Sounds

With regard to spiritual communication, sounds work very similarly to scents and other physical stimuli. The sharpness of individual senses will vary from person to person, so you might garner more meaning from sounds than from scents or tactile sensations. However, keep in mind that the soundscape of the modern world is cluttered with endless interference, so your hearing is more likely to deceive you than most other senses. It's always important to use logic and try to eliminate any worldly explanations before concluding that a spiritual presence is at play. As a channel of spiritual communication, sound will probably work best in the quiet of your meditative space or out in nature, far from the buzzing of urban life.

Sudden Peace

Sudden and pleasantly overwhelming feelings of peace and balance are frequently signs of a benevolent spiritual presence. If you find yourself feeling content, peaceful, and balanced for no discernable reason, it's likely that some kind of spiritual entity is channeling its support to you or is trying to signal that you are on the right path. It can also signify some important breakthrough or spiritual milestone where you or someone you held dear has turned an important corner.

Synchronicities

As you've learned, synchronicities are very important in the world of spirituality. They are a broad yet incredibly consequential category of signs that serve as one of the major avenues of communication for spiritual entities. These entities cannot converse with you clearly and in person, so they will try to get important points across to you via apparent coincidences of all sorts. It's not an accident that the human mind is so sensitive to noticing synchronicities, which makes them difficult to miss. That's why synchronicities are a perfect tool for spiritual entities who want to get your attention. As always, your analyses and interpretations of these signs will unlock the hidden meaning behind them. Pay close attention to those synchronicities that seem to align perfectly with what you're thinking, intending, or doing at a given time, as this can be a clear sign that you are on a good course.

Temperature Changes

Like sounds and fragrances, peculiar shifts in temperature are a solid indication of some sort of presence. As always, don't interpret this as a sign of paranormal activity or anything else that you might consider menacing. As discussed, spirit guides will rarely, if ever, materialize in a physical form, but their energies can sometimes be so intense that they leave physical albeit subtle trails in the world. This is especially true if a strange temperature change occurs indoors where the effects of weather will be minimal and certainly insufficient to dramatically alter the ambient temperature at a moment's notice.

Thoughts

Your thoughts are an area worthy of exploration when it comes to identifying spiritual messages. As much as you might have control over your thoughts from a rational point of view, it's sometimes difficult to be sure about the exact seed from which a certain thought has sprouted. Most of all, it's a good idea to try and analyze the patterns you might observe in your thinking. Doing this without biases and subjectivity is easier said than done, so a journal can be of great help. You should pay particular attention to any recurrent thoughts that seem to come back frequently or any thought loops you often find yourself in.

Visions in Dreams

As you've learned, dreams play a major role in spiritual communication because they provide a canvas for all manner of spiritual messaging. Dream journaling and interpretation are all but essential if you are to unlock the true meaning behind the messages you receive from the spiritual realm. Visible symbols, people, and other living creatures are especially noteworthy motifs to analyze and interpret with regard to messages, although most other aspects of dreams can also be important for other purposes.

Visions in General

Any kind of waking vision, whether subtle or overt, is very likely to be a spirit message. Visions often come from your subconscious mind, but keep in mind that spiritual communication relies heavily on intuition. A vision coming from within doesn't mean that it's not being facilitated by an outside energy or spiritual presence. Visions can be enlightening experiences that reveal important truths and answers in your life, so they should always be analyzed and, ideally, recorded in some form.

Conclusion

The point to really take home is that spirit guides aren't there to take command or appear before you and tell you what you should do with your life. You must understand that spiritual communication shouldn't even be seen as a form of direct conversation in any sense. While spirit guides are certainly entities that operate outside of you, communicating with them actually boils down to looking deep into yourself. Their messages are there to help those who are already on a spiritual path, and the answers contained in those messages will emerge in a person's mind and heart. This means that despite the fact that the messages come from outside, they are read by looking inward.

The same holds true even for those signs and messages that you can directly see, whether they come through animals or inanimate objects in the physical world. These things are there for you to observe, but interpreting them can only be done through introspection and via your own intuition. It might be a strange concept to wrap your head around at first, but once you stop anthropomorphizing the spirit guides, it will quickly dawn on you.

This book has taught you about the different forms of spirit guides, how they operate, and how you can become more mindful of their messages directed at you and all of humanity. Beyond that, you'll have to explore the recesses of your own spirit, mind, and life if you are to get the most out of spiritual communication. With enough reflection and spiritual effort on your part, you will find that a moderate amount of spiritual guidance and a slight nudge in the right direction was all you ever needed in the first place. The knowledge that there are benevolent spirits hovering around you and other people at all times will further reassure you and inspire confidence in your ability to get over grief, find peace, prosper, and place your feet firmly on the right path.

If you enjoyed this book, I'd greatly appreciate a review on Amazon because it helps me to create more books that people want. It would mean a lot to hear from you.

To leave a review:
1. Open your camera app.
2. Point your mobile device at the QR code.
3. The review page will appear in your web browser.

Thanks for your support!

Here's another book by Mari Silva that you might like

Your Free Gift
(only available for a limited time)

Thanks for getting this book! If you want to learn more about various spirituality topics, then join Mari Silva's community and get a free guided meditation MP3 for awakening your third eye. This guided meditation mp3 is designed to open and strengthen ones third eye so you can experience a higher state of consciousness. Simply visit the link below the image to get started.

https://spiritualityspot.com/meditation

Or, Scan the QR code!

References

8 Types Of Spirit Guides & How To Communicate With Them. (2023). Tony Womersley. https://www.tonywomersley.com/blogs/8-types-of-spirit-guides-how-to-communicate-with-them/

A Complete Guide to Psychic Protection and Psychic Self-Defense. (2024, April 18). https://www.psychicsource.com/article/other-psychic-topics/a-complete-guide-to-psychic-protection-and-psychic-self-defense/24918

Alan. (2022, February 14). The 7 Different Types Of Spirit Guides - Subconscious Servant. Subconscious Servant - Mindfulness, Spirituality & Self-Care. https://subconsciousservant.com/types-of-spirit-guides/

Allen, S. (2024, May 12). A Guide to Mediumship Symbols and Signs . Susan Allen Medium. https://susanallenmedium.com/a-guide-to-mediumship-symbols-and-signs/

Anima Mundi Herbals. (2021, May 11). What are Spirit Guides? And How Do You Communicate with Them? Anima Mundi Herbals. https://animamundiherbals.com/blogs/blog/what-are-spirit-guides-and-how-do-you-communicate-with-them

Animal Guides, Totems, Symbolism, Messengers and Meaning. (2015, September). Beautifulgroovyawesomegreat. https://beautifulgroovyawesomegreat.com/2015/09/01/animal-guides-totems-symbolism-messengers-and-meaning/

Aura Health Team. (2023). White Light Meditation: Embrace Purity and Clarity with White Light Meditation. Aura. https://www.aurahealth.io/blog/white-light-meditation

Bartlett, J. (2018, April 6). Symbols as Messages from Spirit, Your Loved Ones and Your Inner Self. Jeaux Bartlett.

https://www.alightintuition.com/intuition/the-signs-and-symbols-you-get-from-spirit/

Beckler, M. (2016, January 16). Angel Numbers – Learn the Angel Number Meanings Today. Ask-Angels.com. https://www.ask-angels.com/spiritual-guidance/angels-and-numbers/

Beckler, M. (2016, September 23). Who Is Your Guardian Angel? And How Can You Connect With Them? Ask-Angels.com. https://www.ask-angels.com/spiritual-guidance/who-is-your-guardian-angel/

Beckler, M. (2019, December 2). Angel Signs ~ 13 Signs Your Angels Are With You! Ask-Angels.com. https://www.ask-angels.com/spiritual-guidance/angel-signs/

Beckler, M. (2020, July 5). 7 Types of Spirit Guides - Which Are On Your Spiritual Team? Ask-Angels.com. https://www.ask-angels.com/spiritual-guidance/types-of-spirit-guides/

Bell, A. (2017, April 15). 9 Most Common Signs of Communication from Spirit | Angie Bell Spiritual Medium. Angie Bell Spiritual Medium | Spiritual Guidance. https://angiebell.com/9-most-common-signs-of-communication-from-spirit/

Belsito, T. (2017, August 17). 12 Common Signs Spirits Send Us to Let Us Know They Are Around! Medium. https://medium.com/@tonybelsito/12-common-signs-spirits-send-us-to-let-us-know-they-are-around-98890b34db87

Carter-King, B. (2018, December 4). What is a Spirit Animal | Spirit Animal vs Totem Animal vs Power Animal. What Is My Spirit Animal. https://whatismyspiritanimal.com/what-is-a-spirit-animal-and-whats-the-difference-between-a-spirit-animal-vs-totem-vs-power-animal/

Desirée. (2023, May 8). The Difference Between Animal Spirits, Guides + Totems. Mojave + Wolf. https://www.mojaveandwolf.com/the-blog/difference-between-animal-guides-spirits-and-totems

Detchon, A. (2018, June 11). The Importance of Grounding and Protecting Your Energy. Linkedin.com. https://www.linkedin.com/pulse/importance-grounding-protecting-your-energy-andrea-detchon-bsc-

Drake, M. (2019). Journey To Meet Your Power Animal. Blogspot.com. https://shamanicdrumming.blogspot.com/2019/11/journey-to-meet-your-power-animal.html?utm_source=chatgpt.com

Embracing Shamanism. (2023, August 15). How Does Shamanism Relate to Nature and Ecology? Embracing Shamanism. https://www.embracingshamanism.org/2023/08/how-does-shamanism-relate-to-nature-and-ecology/

Ferreira, D. (2024, October 5). Angel Messages: How to Receive Them and What They Mean. AskAstrology. https://askastrology.com/life/angel-messages-how-to-receive-them-and-what-they-mean/

Franklin, S. (2023, November 17). The 4 Clairs and How They Are Used in an Intuitive Reading. Intuitive Coaching. https://www.samintuitivecoach.com/post/the-4-clairs

Fraser, M. (2022, February 18). The Most Common Signs From Spirit. Meet Matt Fraser. https://meetmattfraser.com/the-most-common-signs-from-spirit/

Gaia Staff. (2014). 3 Spirit Animal Meditations: Contact Your Animal Guide | Gaia. Gaia. https://www.gaia.com/article/3-spirit-animal-meditations

Greenlaw, F. (2018, December 28). What are Spirit Guides? 5 Things Everybody Gets Wrong. The Wellness Foundry. https://wellnessfoundry.co.uk/what-are-spirit-guides/

Jordan. (2024, September 11). Spirited Earthling. Spirited Earthling. https://www.spiritedearthling.com/mindfulness-and-meditation/helpful-basic-spiritual-protection-practices-you-need-to-know

Journey, T. E. (2024, April 27). Animal Spirit Guides: Finding Your Totem Animal. The Enlightenment Journey. https://theenlightenmentjourney.com/animal-spirit-guides-finding-your-totem-animal/

Kaiser, S. (2022, March 30). 4 Exercises to Build Trust and Confidence in... | Spirituality+Health. Spirituality+Health. https://www.spiritualityhealth.com/4-exercises-to-build-trust-and-confidence-in-your-intuition?utm_source=chatgpt.com

Keen Editorial Staff. (2016). Psychic Advice and Meditation Aid Connection With Spirit Animals - Keen Articles. Keen.com. https://www.keen.com/articles/psychic/psychic-advice-and-meditation-aid-connection-with-spirit-animals

Kleiman, D. (2024, September 19). Myths Busted: The Truth About Spirit Guides No One Tells You - Dina Kleiman - Energy Healer, Intuitive Reader, Spiritual Teacher. Dina Kleiman - Energy Healer, Intuitive Reader, Spiritual Teacher. https://dinakleiman.com/myths-busted-the-truth-about-spirit-guides-no-one-tells-you/

Kulick, D. (2021, August 12). Angels, Spirit Guides, Ancestors: Are Souls of the Dead Watching over Us? | Something to Think About. Pocono Record. https://www.poconorecord.com/story/lifestyle/columns/2021/08/12/angels-spirit-guides-ancestors-souls-dead-watching-us/5556392001/

Lather, K. (2022, April 26). Spirit Guides & Guardian Angels. Angel Connections. https://www.angelconnections.com.au/blog/spirit-guides-amp-guardian-angels

ledbysource. (2019, September 8). Third Eye Visualization. Ledbysource. https://ledbysource.com/third-eye-visualization/

Linette, A. (2014, September 9). Light Spirits: What's The Difference Between Guardian Angels & Spirit Guides? Amanda Linette Meder. https://www.amandalinettemeder.com/blog/2014/9/9/light-spirits-what-is-the-difference-between-guardian-angels-and-spirit-guides

Mills, A. (2024, September 11). Common Signs & Symbols From Loved Ones In Spirit. Arlene Mills. https://arlenemills.com/common-signs-symbols-from-loved-ones-in-spirit/

Monahan, J. B. (2018, June 18). Spiritual Messages and Experiences – Getting, Interpreting and Encouraging More. Medium. https://medium.com/@jennifermonahan_28426/spiritual-messages-and-experiences-getting-interpreting-and-encouraging-more-6fa2b8332d99

Mysticsense. (2020, June 24). What Are Angel Cards and How to Use Them | Mysticsense. Mysticsense. https://www.mysticsense.com/articles/oracle-cards/angel-cards-and-how-to-use-them/

Nicholson, S. (2014). 10 Signs That Spirit Is Trying to Communicate with You. Suenicholson.co.nz. https://www.suenicholson.co.nz/blog/10-signs-that-spirit-is-trying-to-communicate-with-you/

North, S. (2023, September 30). Demystifying Spirit Guides: The Truth About Their Role and Origins. Medium; Heart Speak. https://medium.com/heart-speak/demystifying-spirit-guides-the-truth-about-their-role-and-origins-e69392394858

Pavlina, E. (2011, August 4). What are the Four Clairs of Psychic Ability? • Erin Pavlina, Intuitive Counselor. Erin Pavlina, Intuitive Counselor. https://www.erinpavlina.com/blog/2011/08/what-are-the-four-clairs-of-psychic-ability/

Pearce, J. (2020, March 9). 5 Ways To Connect With Your Guardian Angels. Mindbodygreen.com. https://www.mindbodygreen.com/articles/ways-to-connect-with-guardian-angels

Pearce, K. (2023, April 18). 10 Mindful Walking And Nature Connection Practices. Mindful Ecotourism. https://www.mindfulecotourism.com/the-art-of-mindful-walking-meditation-practices/

Rankin, L. (2015, March 4). 18 Ways To Strengthen Your Intuition. Mindbodygreen. https://www.mindbodygreen.com/articles/how-to-strengthen-your-intuition

Reality Pathing. (2025). 3 Simple Chakrubs Techniques for Daily Energy Alignment | Reality Pathing. Realitypathing.com. https://realitypathing.com/3-simple-chakrubs-techniques-for-daily-energy-alignment/

Redford, N. (2024, October 18). Animal Spirit Oracle Cards: Unlocking Intuition and Emotional Guidance for Personal Growth. The Indie Spiritualist. https://theindiespiritualist.com/animal-spirit-oracle-cards/

Reiss, A. (2023, March 24). 4 Types of Spirits That Departed Loved Ones Become | California Psychics. California Psychics. https://www.californiapsychics.com/blog/psychic-tools-abilities/medium/spirits-departed-loved-ones-become.html

Richardson, T. C. (2017, June 13). How To Use Your Intuition Like A Professional Psychic. Mindbodygreen. https://www.mindbodygreen.com/articles/the-4-types-of-intuition-and-how-to-tap-into-each

Romano, A. (2024, January 30). Master Simple Techniques for Manifestation and Energy Alignment. Affirm Your Reality. https://affirmyourreality.com/simple-techniques-for-energy-alignment-in-manifestation/

Runa Heilung. (2024, January 8). Journey to Meet Your Spirit Animal - Old Soul Alchemy - Medium. Medium; Old Soul Alchemy. https://medium.com/old-soul-alchemy/journey-to-meet-your-spirit-animal-70d57455984e

Samford, L. (2022, June 14). Walking Nature Meditation for Deeper Connection. Lena Samford. https://lenasamford.com/walking-nature-meditation-for-deeper-connection/

Sara. (2024). Connect With Your Spirit Guide, Meditation Script. Letsmovemindfully.com. https://letsmovemindfully.com/meet-your-spirit-guide/

Sayce, A. (2021, June). Can Deceased Loved Ones Become Our Spirit Guides After They Pass? Anna Sayce. https://annasayce.com/can-deceased-loved-ones-become-our-spirit-guides-after-they-pass/

Signs from the Universe. (2025, January 18). How to Identify Your Nature Spirit Guide. Signsfromtheuniverse.guide. https://signsfromtheuniverse.guide/how-to-identify-your-nature-spirit-guide/

Snyder, K. (2022, January 25). Looking for Stronger Intuition? Try This Third Eye Meditation. Yoga Journal. https://www.yogajournal.com/meditation/third-eye-meditation-for-intuition/

Sun. (2024, May 19). Rooted Sun. Rooted Sun. https://www.rootedsun.co/blog/11-simple-exercises-to-unlock-your-third-eye

The Enlightenment Journey. (2023, June 18). Psychic Self-Defense: Techniques and Strategies - The Enlightenment Journey - Medium. Medium; Medium. https://medium.com/@tej88/psychic-self-defense-techniques-and-strategies-d62fcee2eff4

The Enlightenment Journey. (2024, August 17). How to Use Meditation and Visualization with Ascended Masters. The Enlightenment Journey. https://theenlightenmentjourney.com/how-to-use-meditation-and-visualization-with-ascended-masters/

The Enlightenment Journey. (2024, May 15). Types Of Spirit Guides: Finding Your Spiritual Allies. The Enlightenment Journey. https://theenlightenmentjourney.com/types-of-spirit-guides-finding-your-spiritual-allies/

The Enlightenment Journey. (2024, October 5). Connecting with Your Guardian Angel. The Enlightenment Journey. https://theenlightenmentjourney.com/connecting-with-your-guardian-angel/

The Enlightenment Journey. (2024a, April 27). Fairy Spirit Guides: Communicating with Nature's Spirits. The Enlightenment Journey. https://theenlightenmentjourney.com/fairy-spirit-guides-communicating-with-natures-spirits/

The Enlightenment Journey. (2024b, April 27). Nature Spirit Guides: Channeling Earthly Energies. The Enlightenment Journey. https://theenlightenmentjourney.com/nature-spirit-guides-channeling-earthly-energies/

The Enlightenment Journey. (2024c, June 6). Elemental Spirits: Earth, Air, Fire, Water. The Enlightenment Journey. https://theenlightenmentjourney.com/elemental-spirits-earth-air-fire-water/

The Reforest Nation Team. (2023, February 5). Nature & Folklore: An Interwoven Legacy in Ireland. Reforest Nation. https://www.reforestnation.ie/blog/nature-folklore-an-interwoven-legacy-in-ireland

Tully, S. (2023, January 24). How To Connect To Spirit Guides – Sonia. Soniatully.com. https://soniatully.com/2023/01/24/how-to-connect-to-spirit-guides/

Webster, R. (2022, June 13). 7 Ways to Connect with Archangels. Llewellyn Worldwide, Ltd. https://www.llewellyn.com/journal/article/3023

Wicked Obscura. (2024, August 29). Signs That Your Spirit Guides Are Trying to Communicate with You. Wicked Obscura Apothecary. https://www.wickedobscura.com/blog/2024/8/29/signs-that-your-spirit-guides-are-trying-to-communicate-with-you

Wolf, M. (2022, March 27). 6 - The Intuitive Nudge - Path of Courage. Path of Courage. https://pathofcourage.com/the-intuitive-nudge/

Your Higher Journey. (2021, February 15). What Are Ascended Masters? This Guide Explains All Your Higher Journey. https://www.yourhigherjourney.com/numerology/what-are-ascended-masters/

Image Sources

1. Designed by Freepik. https://www.freepik.com/free-photo/numerology-concept-with-woman-posing_41252224.htm
2. https://www.pexels.com/photo/an-eagle-flying-in-the-sky-3250638/
3. https://www.pexels.com/photo/a-woman-engaged-in-fortune-telling-6944681/
4. https://www.pexels.com/photo/woman-sitting-on-brown-stone-near-green-leaf-trees-at-daytime-1234035/
5. Designed by Freepik. https://www.freepik.com/free-vector/body-chakras-concept_8515104.htm
6. https://www.pexels.com/photo/woman-closing-her-eyes-against-sun-light-standing-near-purple-petaled-flower-plant-321576/
7. https://www.freepik.com/free-photo/brown-eye-bright-background_31499094.htm
8. Designed by Freepik. https://www.freepik.com/free-psd/cartoon-angel-wings-isoltated_178832496.htm
9. https://www.pexels.com/photo/gray-feather-on-tree-stem-394376/
10. https://www.freepik.com/free-photo/overhead-view-eyes-closed-woman-lying-near-open-blank-book-blanket_5233812.htm
11. https://www.pexels.com/photo/white-and-black-wolf-397857/
12. https://www.pexels.com/photo/woman-in-black-top-sitting-on-brown-armchair-3331574/
13. Designed by Freepik. https://www.freepik.com/free-vector/animals-black-linocut-stencil-pattern-drawing-collection_16338492.htm
14. https://www.pexels.com/photo/worms-eyeview-of-green-trees-957024/
15. https://www.pexels.com/photo/woman-sleeping-935777/

16 https://www.pexels.com/photo/photo-of-person-standing-on-grass-2623878/
17 Designed by Freepik. https://www.freepik.com/free-photo/abstract-numerology-concept-with-man-seaside_36300065.htm
18 Designed by Freepik. https://www.freepik.com/free-vector/snihy-star-background_1177943.htm
19 https://www.pexels.com/photo/materials-for-witchcraft-and-burning-candles-on-a-round-table-7189446/
20 https://www.pexels.com/photo/close-up-shot-of-fortune-telling-objects-7221573/
21 https://www.pexels.com/photo/photo-of-person-holding-cup-3363111/
22 https://www.freepik.com/free-photo/young-girl-meditate-green-forest-with-sunlight_3952256.htm
23 https://www.pexels.com/photo/woman-meditating-with-candles-and-incense-3822864/

Printed in Great Britain
by Amazon